James Maclaren Cobban

The Burden of Isabel

Vol. 1

James Maclaren Cobban

The Burden of Isabel
Vol. 1

ISBN/EAN: 9783337779757

Printed in Europe, USA, Canada, Australia, Japan

Cover: Foto ©ninafisch / pixelio.de

More available books at **www.hansebooks.com**

THE
BURDEN OF ISABEL

BY

J. MACLAREN COBBAN

AUTHOR OF 'THE RED SULTAN' 'MASTER OF HIS FATE' ETC.

IN THREE VOLUMES

VOL. I.

London

CHATTO & WINDUS, PICCADILLY

1893

TO

JOHN RUSSELL

WHOSE EXPERIENCE AND COUNSEL WERE OF MUCH AVAIL

IN THE CONSTRUCTION OF THIS STORY

CONTENTS

OF

THE FIRST VOLUME

CHAPTER   PAGE

   I. THE RETURN OF THE MASTER . . . 1

  II. UNCLE HARRY 25

 III. THE BLACK TULIP AND THE LILY OF THE
VALLEY 49

  IV. THE TAME PHILOSOPHER 61

   V. ISABEL'S LETTER 79

  VI. ALAN AINSWORTH 94

 VII. HOW AINSWORTH SOLVED HIS PROBLEM . . 103

VIII. AT THE GREAT WHITE FEAST . . . 128

  IX. WHAT CAME OF A LECTURE AT THE ROYAL
GEOGRAPHICAL 154

   X. THE ONLY WOMAN IN THE WORLD . . . 174

  XI. MR. DOUGHTY EXPLAINS 191

 XII. A PRODIGAL FATHER 214

XIII. SAHIB GEORGE 233

XIV. THE FATTED CALF. 250

 XV. PLANS AND PROSPECTS . . . 277

THE
BURDEN OF ISABEL

CHAPTER I

THE RETURN OF THE MASTER

To the æsthetically minded, Southern Lancashire is the most provoking and irritating region within the coasts of Great Britain. It constantly suggests that there might have been unrivalled opportunities for delight in the picturesque and the beautiful, had they not been hewn away, trampled on, or covered up by the remorseless genius of modern Lancashire industry. Here, for instance, is a glen which Nature intended to be as romantic as any in the north, with birch-clothed sides, a clear and frolicsome trout-stream, and turf as soft and scented as the mead of Asphodel. Nature's intention, however, has been thwarted, and before us are merely a convenient hollow and convenient water for dye-works: the sky-line is cut by a tall smoking chimney; the upper end of the glen is blocked by a pile of buildings and a dirty dam; the birches are stunted and blighted by smoke and the gases of filthy chemicals; the stream is choked by ashes and other refuse, and is shrunk to an ashamed and noisome dribble; and the mead of Asphodel is turned into a broad cinder-track for mill-hands and coal-carts. That is a common and saddening sight in Southern Lancashire. Yet are there others where it is pleasant and cheering to see that, under proper and kindly control, the genius of modern industry may have room and verge enough without committing outrage of a wanton kind upon dear Mother Nature. Not very far from the glen (or clough) already indicated there is another—or *was*, a few years ago—where Nature had not been outraged, but only tamed a little. There also were chimney-shafts and buildings and a dam ; but the chimneys were notably tall, so that smoke and acrid vapours were carried far above the glen ; the buildings were half-hid by healthy and stalwart elms, and smothered with ivy and flowering creepers ; and the dam looked like a natural lake, its wholesome waters being inhabited by fish and water-fowl, and by the homely duck and the stately swan, and its shady banks overgrown with flags and meadow-sweet. There the stream was clear, and frolicked gaily along at its own sweet will, flashing over pebbles and circumventing obstructive boulders, or boldly dashing over them. There, too, the turf was turf, green and sweet, where children romped of an afternoon, lads and lasses walked of an evening, and fairies even danced o' nights to the amazement of the prick-eared, half-tame rabbits. And the kindly arranger and controller of all this was George Suffield, cotton-spinner and calico-printer, and Member of Parliament.

On a certain night late in May, Mr. Suffield was walking along the brink of the glen on a foot-path that led from the station. He was returning from a sedulous attention to the legislation of the country to enjoy the brief vacation of Whitsuntide in the bosom of his family. It was very late—almost midnight, indeed—but a full moon illumined all the scene with a pale mystic light—the clough, the park beyond it, with the Hall, towards which its master was making his way, and the village before him with its neat cottages and gardens and its church standing white in the moonlight with its tower and its tapering spire. Suffield walked like a man well pleased with himself and his kind, bearing his bulging Gladstone bag, as he did his years, lightly. He was a man of sixty or more, but he was what is called ' well preserved.' His hair and beard were grizzled, that is to say ; but, while tall and strongly built, he was straight and ruddy, and he showed a fine, careless, open front to the world. Whether the influence of the moon or the neighbourhood of the fairies of the clough had touched him, he was in a light and vacant mood. He did not whistle as he went 'for want of thought;' but he hummed little catches to himself, and quoted to himself random scraps from his random reading. The tower of the church which he had built caught his roving eye, and he quoted—not too correctly—

> They built up the tower of Jumley-Jee.
> They built it up to a goodly height
> At eleven o'clock on a Thursday night.

'Why Thursday night ?' he asked himself,

with a low chuckle of enjoyment of the absurdity of the thing. 'And why on earth at eleven o'clock? Ah, well; I suppose it was just meant to make you laugh; and it does.'

Thus he walked leisurely along, enjoying the soft night-air, enjoying the moonlight, enjoying the fair rich scene spread before him, and enjoying above all the sense that he had become the possessor and controller of all he saw by his own effort. He came of an obscure but sturdy and honest stock. His father had been a farmer and weaver ' back o' th' White Moss,' in the easy old days before Lancashire industry had become so enormous, congested, and reckless. His parents had given him a sound body and a shrewd head, a large heart and a small education, and by the help of God and of a resolute purpose— and, it must be added, of a good wife, whom he adored—he had done the rest himself.

Note him well; for he was of a generation that is fast passing away, a generation whose sons seem to lack much of the old Lancashire 'grit,' and the cheery and intrepid energy that set England in the front rank of the commerce and the humanity of the world.

As he continued his placid way, suddenly there came from the clough beneath him, and, it seemed to him, from a spot not far off, the squeak of a scared or captured rabbit, and close upon it a soothing and satisfied 'Wirroo!'

'A poacher! The rascal!' exclaimed Suffield to himself.

Without a moment's hesitation, he set down his bag and slipped over the brow of the clough. He had but turned a hillock when, in the shade of two or three birches, he saw a creature in white—man or woman, he could not tell which—kneeling on the ground and holding a struggling rabbit by the ears.

'Put that beast down!' cried Suffield.

'Ow!' exclaimed the creature, at once dropping the rabbit, which bounded away and disappeared in a hole.

'And who the dickens are you to come poaching here?' demanded Suffield. 'Stand up and show yourself.'

The creature in white stood up, and came softly forward into the full moonlight. Suffield was amazed to see the creature resolve itself into a black man with very bright eyes and white teeth, and wearing a big white turban, a kind of white blouse with an ample red sash, and trousers of some dark material. The black man made a profound obeisance with his black hands crossed upon his white breast.

'Respectable sir,' he murmured in a very soft voice. He said no more, but bowed still lower and slowly shook his head, as if to deprecate the white man's anger.

'Where on earth do you come from?' said Suffield. 'Art a boggart?' he demanded, lapsing into dialect, 'or a kind o' demon fro' th' pit?'

'Respectable sir, no,' answered the black man. 'To speak with regards to your terms, I am not a demon, etcetera. I am Daniel—at your kind, respectable services.'

'What?' laughed Suffield, with a pleasant reminiscence in his mind of the judge in 'Pickwick.' 'Daniel Nathaniel, or Nathaniel Daniel?'

'Respectable sir, no,' answered Daniel; 'I am Daniel Trichinopoly. The same time I must say I am servant, dressing-boy, and cook, and have answered to several others' capacity as clerk, store-keeper, etcetera, etcetera, to a gentleman staying at the great Hall, namely, the Sahib Raynor.'

'Oh, ah!' exclaimed Suffield. 'You're

Mr. Raynor's black servant. But why couldn't you say that in so many words?'

'Respectable sir,' answered Daniel, 'I am regret to say that I have said it in so many words as I was able.'

'Ah,' said Suffield, with a laugh, 'I make no doubt you have.—Well, Daniel, your master has arrived, then? When did he come? To-day?'

'Respectable sir,' answered Daniel, still with mellifluous precision, 'if care should be taken to be true the Sahib Raynor arrived the day before to-day.'

'But you haven't told me, Daniel, how you came to be snaring my rabbits. The rabbits are mine, you know; I am Mr. Suffield.'

'Ah, respectable sir, you are indeed the Sahib Suffield? Large and splendid sir, I kiss your hem;' and he was about to carry his salutation into effect.

'No, no, man; don't do that,' said Suffield hurriedly; for he had the English shame of homage of that grovelling sort. 'Stand up and tell me why you were snaring my rabbits: *we* call it poaching.'

'Poaching!' Daniel accepted the word with a supple bow. 'Now, I must say I am taking myself a walk in the scenery, and I am thinking nicely of the moon of India; the same time my sharp eye see a little wild beast run, and I am say to myself: "The little wild beast is made to catch and cook. I am intention to catch and cook and curry him for my master, the Sahib Raynor, etcetera." With regards, large and splendid sir,' said Daniel, with another humble obeisance, 'I hope I am forgive for my own experience. I am just come the day before to-day, and I am still not learned in the manners, customs, ways, etcetera.'

'But, Daniel,' said Suffield, very much

interested and amused, 'I thought a Hindu, or Buddhist—I don't know which you are—was forbidden by his religion to catch and kill any beast.'

'Large and splendid sir,' said Daniel, in an energy of resentment, 'with regard to above I am not Hindu, I am not Buddhist : I am Chlistian like my master !'

'H'm, ha,' said Suffield, struck by the reply; 'you've had me there. I suppose that *is* answer enough—that you are Christian—like your master. You've learned your Christian lesson well. And, now, you're going back to my house, I suppose, Daniel? Let us walk on together.'

'Large and splendid sir,' said Daniel, making another obeisance with his dingy hands crossed on his white breast, 'I will be highly thankful.'

'God made man upright,' said Suffield to himself, 'but he will bow and wriggle.'

So they climbed out of the clough and returned to find Mr. Suffield's bag, which Daniel insisted on carrying; and thus they went on their way through the village, past the works, round the head of the clough, across the stream by a pretty rustic bridge, and into the park properly so-called. The park was extensive, and the house—Holdsworth Hall—stood on a gentle eminence about half a mile from the works and the village. Mr. Suffield and his strange companion, therefore, had plenty of time to become acquainted with each other. Suffield was one of those of whom Sir Walter Scott approved, who act, consciously or unconsciously, on the great Roman writer's rule—' nihil humani a me alienum puto '—who are familiar and sympathetic, that is to say, with all sorts and conditions of men, and who think no human creature too humble, too stupid, too ignorant, or too foreign to teach them something.

From the dusky Daniel—who, closer at hand and in the fuller light, was seen to be not black, but rather brown or coffee-coloured —he learned, what he already knew fairly well, that cotton-spinning and weaving and calico-printing were rapidly becoming great industries about Bombay; moreover, that Daniel himself when a very young man had worked in a cotton-mill, and that he had a longing to become better acquainted with cotton-manufacture in general, because he believed —had he not evidence at his elbow in support of his belief?—that that way splendour and fortune lay. It was a memorable conversation, though, like most things memorable, it became so only in the light of subsequent events—events which appertain to this story.

'It's late; you'd better come in this way,' said Suffield, when they had reached the great hall door. 'Some of the family up, I see: there's light in the dining-room.'

He knocked and rang a loud peal, and a young gentleman in evening dress and a sleepy-looking elderly servant in knee-breeches came to open the door together. Both appeared a little surprised to see the strange companion the master of the house had got.

'Oh, Trichy,' said the young man, *passim*, 'you're out late.'

'Yes, Sahib George,' grinned Daniel—he had clearly got into the way already of regarding 'Sahib' George as an amusing person—'I appear to be.'

'Well, father,' said George, grasping the paternal hand, 'you've come home at last.'

'Yea, lad,' said Suffield; 'and right glad I am to be out o' that big, roaring London. —And how's things?'

'All right, dad.'

It was good to see the looks of affection

and confidence that passed between father and son.

'And how's Tummas?' called Suffield after the elderly man-servant, who was retiring in Daniel's company.

'Pretty bobbish, mester,' answered Tummas, 'as the sayin' is.'

'That's all right,' said Suffield. Then in a low voice he remarked to his son: 'He was going away looking rather disappointed. He thought, I suppose, I had forgotten him, poor owd Tummas!—Is your mother up?'

'No,' answered George, 'mother has gone to bed.'

'And Uncle Harry?'

'He has gone to bed too,' said George. 'The rest of us have been to the theatre.'

'Oh, it's father!' cried a charming young lady, jumping up and running to Suffield the moment he showed himself in the dining-room.

'Yes, my lass,' said he, taking her in his arms—she was small and slight, though shapely—'it *is* feyther. And here's Cousin Isabel too.'

A tall, dark, and strikingly handsome young lady, who had stood waiting with a smile for her turn to be saluted, now came forward. 'I'm here again, you see, uncle,' said she when she had kissed him.

'You can't come too often, my lass,' said Suffield. 'The only mistake you make, as I've told you before, is not to stay here altogether.'

'It's kind of you to say that, uncle, even though you have said it before. But you know I'm an old maid——'

'An old maid!' exclaimed Suffield's daughter, clasping her round the waist. 'Hear her, father! Hear her, George! An old maid at four-and-twenty!'

'Still, my dear,' said Cousin Isabel, 'like

the old gentleman in the play, I protest in the face of Europe that in essence if not in actual fact I *am* an old maid. I have my own queer, solitary ways that I should not like to give up.'

'Well,' said Suffield, 'you must be fonder o' other people's brats than I should be, Isabel, to spend all your days teaching one lot after another—one down, t'other come on.'

'Don't you speak of teaching, uncle,' laughed Isabel, 'rather as if it were fighting?'

'I know I'd rather do the fighting myself. Have you had supper? I think I'll just have a mouthful.'

He sat down to eat and drink, and the others sat about him.

'Well,' said Suffield, 'tell me what you saw at the theatre. Was it in the play to-night, Isabel, that the old gentleman protested in the face of Europe? I like that saying: "protested in the face of Europe," I daresay, when he was standing in his own back-kitchen.'

'Something like that, uncle,' answered Isabel. 'But it was not in the play to-night; it's in a French play.'

'Oh, ah,' said her uncle; 'a French play: Frenchies say that kind o' thing. What was the play, then, to-night?'

George answered his father in some detail. It was notable that he had not spoken till then, that while Cousin Isabel had been excusing herself, he had appeared uneasy, not to say impatient and hurt, and that he had cast on her several appealing looks, of which she had remained either unconscious or regardless. About the quality of the play and the players the young people did not agree. Both play and players were London successes—a fact which seemed to subdue what critical judgment the easy and good-natured George

possessed : like most of the younger generation, he believed in all things metropolitan ;
he had his coats, his hats, and his boots made
in London; his favourite reading was the
London papers ; and he was constantly 'running up to town.' His sister, Euphemia, did not
even affect to be critical ; she bubbled over with
direct, unthinking enthusiasm, and thought
everything she had seen—especially the
dresses—'quite too lovely.' Cousin Isabel,
on the other hand, was not only critical, but
—it seemed to the others—irreverent and
revolutionary. She not only called the play
a vulgar travesty of a noble story, but laughed
at the silly sentimentalism and the mean and
jerky elocution with which the parts had been
rendered ; moreover, she declared that, if such
things continued to be generally admired and
praised, the theatre would be as little worth
going to as a 'penny reading.' These
opinions unutterably disturbed the three

Suffields, whose only doubt hitherto had been that the theatre was not morally beyond reproach.　And yet they could not ignore or despise what she said ; for, apart from the fact that all three were fond of her, they all believed in her cleverness and her judgment, and in her prescriptive right to be severely critical of all things : was she not—though of their family—a teacher in a celebrated Ladies' College in London, and by that token a kind of animate encyclopædia of knowledge?

'Ah, well,' said the benign Suffield, summing up and closing the discussion, 'you're beyond me, Isabel.　You strike a high note that I can't reach—a very high note indeed. But tell me—did any of you see Ainsworth there?'

'Of course,' answered the brother and sister together ; 'he was there for the paper.'

'That's all right,' said their father.　'He'll

settle it for us. We'll see what he says about it in the morning's paper.'

'He won't go against the verdict of London,' said George.

'Oh, won't he?' said his father. 'Perhaps he won't and perhaps he will; but it won't depend on what he cares for what they say or what they think in London. I doubt very much if there's any writer on the London papers cleverer than himself, or as clever. He has a fine head on him, has Alan; he's half Scots and half Lancashire, and he'll go far.—You remember Ainsworth—don't you, Isabel? He's dramatic critic and all the rest of it for the *Gazette*.'

'Oh yes,' said Isabel, 'I remember Mr. Ainsworth.'

'Well, now,' said her uncle, looking at his watch, 'it's time we all went to bed.'

When the girls withdrew, he and George went round to see that all doors and shutters were secured, and then ascending to their rooms, they said 'good-night' at the top of the stairs. But on his way to his own room Suffield observed that the door of the great spare room stood open, where, he imagined, Uncle Harry, the 'Sahib' Raynor, was put up. He looked into the room, and discovered that the bed, though tumbled, was empty. In perplexity and alarm, he called his son softly.

'This is Uncle Harry's room, isn't it?' he asked.

George answered that it was; and he, too, looked in to make sure that Uncle Harry was not playing them a prank; but neither in bed, nor under it, nor in wardrobe or cupboard, could Uncle Harry be found.

'What the dickens can have become of him?' said Suffield. 'Perhaps your mother will know.' He entered his wife's room, and soon returned relieved and chuckling. 'What do you think?' he said to his son. 'Your mother tells me he's camping out! He has been so many years used to sleeping out o' doors, that he can't be comfortable in a proper bed and a proper bedroom, and he begged your mother to let him take a blanket out into the park! He's a caution; but I'll find him i' th' morning.'

CHAPTER II

UNCLE HARRY

VERY early next morning Mr. Suffield himself opened his hall door and inhaled the fresh morning air with a loud and satisfied 'Ah!' He left the hall door open—to have all things belonging to him open was characteristic of the excellent man—and sauntered away through the park, with his hands in his pockets, whistling softly to himself, and cocking now and then a half-observant eye on the trees and the rooks, that cocked wholly observant eyes on him and cawed, but sat still, as if they also knew all about his openness and hospitality. He sauntered on, and still on, steadily, as if he had a fixed end in view, though he rambled a good deal from a straight line. 'Now, where the dickens has he put himself up?' he said aloud. He looked all around, surveying bit by bit every hollow and every clump of trees in his purview. At length something caught his eye a tolerable way off. 'Ah,' said he cheerfully—regardless of grammar— 'that must be him.' He quickened his pace, and made directly for the object he had descried. As he neared it, he could make it out to be a kind of small tent pitched under a great beech. 'Hah!' he exclaimed to himself. 'That's how he does it.' When he got quite near, he tramped round to examine the disposition of the erection, grunting good-naturedly as he remarked each point, 'Hum! Ha-ha!' He had noted that the ridge-pole of the tent was an almost bare arm of the beech which stuck out at right angles at about the height of a man; that the tent itself was a piece of sailcloth stretched over the bare bough, and pegged to the ground at the interval of a yard or so; and that one end was closed by a triangular flap of cloth, while the other was open, and had evidently had a small fire of dried twigs burning against it. He had noted these things, when he perceived that a corner of the flap was gently raised, showing a face and the shining barrel of a rifle.

'Holloa, Harry!' cried Suffield with a laugh. 'Hold hard! And save your powder!'

Then there came from the tent a chuckle of laughter, followed by a little, wiry-looking man in a complete suit of flannels. A rather remarkable and authoritative little man he seemed, with the dense hair of head and beard close-clipped, and grey and stiff as a badger's, and clear grey eyes keen as a needle. He said not a word, but yawned and stretched his arms.

'Going to have a pot-shot at me, were you?' said Suffield.

'I think,' said the little man, 'I was dreaming I was in the jungles I've come from; and the tramping of your feet and your grunting—you *were* grunting, you know —made me think of an elephant, or some other wild creature.'

'That's all right, Harry. It's just the kind o' thing you'd ha' said five-and-twenty years ago. But what sort of sleep have you had?'

'Capital. The sleep, George, of the natural man, constant, light, and refreshing.'

'Well, Harry,' said Suffield, 'I'd a deal rather you than me. I'm unnatural man enough to prefer a bed and a four-poster in a good big room, with no draughts about. Of course, this sort of thing, the green grass, the open air, " Hail, smiling morn!" and all that, I daresay, suits you—it may suit you in fine weather, at least—but I'd have thought you'd had so much of it in your time, lad, that you'd appreciate the comfort of a regular bed in a proper bedroom. Howsoever, there you are, and here I am, and of course you're free to do as you like. I only heard late last night that you had taken up your traps and camped out. I didn't get home till very late, and the wife was in bed; but she told me that you had found your bed too soft——'

'Abominably soft,' said the other; 'I wallowed in softness.'

'I daresay you did, lad: our beds are all the finest feather-beds, stuffed by the hands of my own blessed mother, and she didn't spare the feathers, I can tell you. Yes, the wife said you had found the bed soft and the room stuffy, even wi' th' windows wide open, and so you had just taken up your bed and walked.'

He paused in his talk to observe his brother-in-law, who had struck his tent, and was rolling it up.

'Ah,' said Suffield, 'you're pretty comfortable after all: a blanket, a carpet, and a pillow.   But what about catching rheumatism, my lad?'

'Underneath my carpet, you see'—he showed him—'is a mackintosh sheet.'

'Ah,' said the interested Suffield, taking up and handling the pillow, 'a kind o' india-rubber bladder, eh? Good idea that, my lad: keeps your head cool.'

'Which, you will perhaps say, George, is not unnecessary.'

'Nay, nay, lad,' said George; 'that's understood: no need to say it.'

'I'm proud of this pillow, though,' said the other, with a laugh. 'It not only keeps my brain cool, but it keeps my mouth cool too.   It's just a pillow now; but it can be a

water-bottle on occasion, and many a time it
has served me as that.'

'That's economical, lad, certainly,' said
Suffield. 'And have you a double use for all
your traps?'

'For most of them,' answered the other.
'This little Persian carpet, now, I use also as
a saddle-cloth.'

'Ah,' said Suffield, 'but your little tent—
what about it?'

'There, now,' said Harry, 'what other
use do you think I put it to?'

'Can't guess,' said Suffield; 'unless you
make your bearers or servants carry it over
you like a canopy.'

'I make a sail of it,' said the other with
a nod of pride. 'You know I carry with me
on my journeys a boat in sections; well,
there I have a sail ready to rig up when I
can.'

''Pon my word, Harry,' said Suffield,

'you're just the same ingenious young rascal as used to fry bacon and boil potatoes and make toffee in the same saucepan at school!'

'And, 'pon my word, George,' exclaimed Harry, 'you're just the same fat, talkative old rascal as used to sit by and criticise my cooking, and then help to eat it!'

At that they both laughed, while the tent-dweller finished packing away his traps. 'I suppose,' said he, 'I can leave them here?'

'Oh, to be sure,' said Suffield. 'There's to be a treat in the park to-day for my hands and the childer; but that don't matter: they'll interfere wi' nought. Set them again the tree, lad—except your blanket; perhaps we'd best carry that in, in case it should rain.'

They sauntered away back towards the house together, Suffield taking his old school-fellow's arm, and insisting on carrying his blanket.

'And how,' asked the old schoolfellow, 'do you get on with your workpeopl in these days of strikes and of Jack in general being as good as his master?'

'I've no trouble,' answered Suffield. 'I treat my people well, and they treat me well. I reckon them more than mere machines to keep my works going, and they reckon me a good master.'

'Ah,' said the other, 'you want to rule with sugar-sticks.'

'I don't want to rule at all, my lad,' said Suffield; 'but if I must rule, I'd rather do it wi' sugar-sticks than wi' cat-o'-nine-tails.'

'Ah, it won't do, George.'

'Well, Harry,' said Suffield, 'we won't discuss it: our point o' view's different. You've been used to black fellows; I've been used to Englishmen. By the way, I came across your black servant last night. There's a deal of human nature in him for a black

man. He had caught a rabbit, which, he
said, he meant to curry for you.'

'I daresay. He *can* curry.'

'I rather like him: an amusing creature.'

'Oh,' said Harry, 'he can curry favour too.'

'Harry, my lad,' said Suffield, 'that's an
old trick of yours—punning. You stick to
your old habits.'

'About the only things old that I do stick
to—except old friends, George.'

'That's as it should be, Harry. But come
now. Tell me about yourself. Have you done
pretty well out there?—what wi' ruby mines
and white elephants and all that sort o' game?'

'Oh yes, pretty well,' answered the other,
shooting a keen glance at Suffield's face.
The glance could not fail to assure him that
there was nothing in the inquiry but kindly
interest, and he repeated less sharply than
before; 'Yes; oh yes, pretty well.'

'And you're come home now to settle

down—I can't say, in your own house—but in your own tent, I hope?'

'Perhaps, perhaps.   I can't say yet.'

'Ah, now, Harry, I want to talk to you,' continued Suffield, 'about Isabel Raynor, your niece—and my niece, of course, too— your poor brother John's daughter.   You've seen her, of course?'

'Oh yes; I've seen her.'

'And a handsome, clever girl she is,' said Suffield.

'Is she?' said Uncle Harry, as if he were little interested in the matter.

'Is she?' echoed Suffield.   'Why, lad, don't you know a handsome woman when you see her, and a clever woman when you talk to her?'

'I'm no judge of women, George. They're not in my line.'

'I see what you would be at, Harry,' said Suffield seriously, after a meditative pause.

'But I had no idea you could keep that feeling up so long. "Let not the sun go down upon. thy wrath," my lad ; but many and many a sun have you let go down. It's not right, Harry ; it's wicked, lad, and you'll rue it yet. Howsoever, you'll come right in the end, I reckon. I believe your heart's in the right place ; and you'll like the girl if you give yourself the chance.'

'I noticed,' said Uncle Harry, 'that your son seems to have given himself a good chance in that way: he appears to like his cousin rather more than .mere cousinship demands.'

'Yes,' said Suffield simply ; 'George thinks a deal of Isabel, and is, I believe, fond of her. A man's best fortune, or his worst, is his wife. I have no doubt which Isabel would be, and I'd like George to have her. But somehow they don't seem to hit it off: she doesn't cotton to him.'

'"Cotton," George, is a good word to use in the connection.'

'I know what you mean, Harry,' said Suffield. 'But this is not a time for joking. I tell you I think about Isabel a great deal. I don't like to know she's working hard at school-keeping, and living in lonely lodgings in London, when we've more than we know what to do with. It's not good for a woman any more than for a man to live alone. I've begged her till my mouth was dry wi' begging to come and stay with us; but, "no," she won't, thank me all the same. Now, if she'd only take on wi' George——'

'"Cotton,"' corrected Uncle Harry with a mischievous smile.

——'and set up house wi' him,' continued the excellent Suffield, as if he had not heard the interruption, 'I should be happy about her.'

'Well, George,' said Uncle Harry, 'she

ought to do a good deal for you : you've done a great deal for her ; though I am prepared to admit that gratitude for kindness is the last return a man should expect.'

'Gratitude, my lad ! I get more of it than I can do with from folk. But gratitude I neither require nor need from Isabel. I've done no more for her than I've done for th' rabbits in th' clough yonder. I've given them the chance of fending for themselves without going in terror of their lives ; and that's all I ever did for Isabel. If she'd take to George—and he's not a bad lad at all—I'd take it, not as gratitude, but as a favour, as a kind of condescension on her part ; for she's handsome and clever, as I said before, and as good a girl as can be.'

'But,' asked Uncle Harry, 'would your wife, my admirable sister, be satisfied ? Hasn't she a greater ambition for her son than that ? '

'Oh, you've noticed that already, have you? Yes, Joanna is chock-full of ambitions for all of us—for me, too, bless her!'

'Well, after all,' said the uncle, 'I don't myself approve of cousins marrying.'

'Not if they're both perfectly healthy? Howsoever, Harry, that just brings me to my point: since it doesn't seem likely that Isabel will take to George, don't you think you might—well, do your duty by her?'

'And what, George,' asked the uncle quietly, 'does a good man like you think my duty?'

'Well, it's hard to say ; but forget what's past, my lad. Do something for the girl: ask her to keep house for you or summat?'

'I don't intend at present, George, to set up house, even if you turn me out.'

'Turn you out! You've turned yourself out, and taken the key of the park.'

'Well, then, my dear George,' said Uncle

Harry, stopping and laying his hand on his brother-in-law's arm, 'we'll not discuss it any more at present.   You're a good man, George, but give me a little time to find where I am. Now, I'm going to have a dip in your stream. The water is pure enough, I suppose?'

'Pure enough to-day to drink if you like.'

'By the way,' said Uncle Harry, 'why are the mills not started yet?   It's past six a long while.'

'Mills started !   You forget it's Whitsuntide.   We're idle for a week.'

They were now on the brink of the glen, which was separated from the park by a low oak paling, with a convenient stile at the point where they had arrived.   While Uncle Harry descended into the glen for his morning dip, Mr. Suffield sat on the stile and meditated. His meditation took the form of reminiscence of his own and Harry Raynor's youth—a memorial excursion on which the few words

they had exchanged about Isabel had set
him off. 'Poor old Harry!' he murmured,
glancing after his brother-in-law. He gradually raised his eyes and let his mental vision
travel over the glen and the clean and cosy
village he had built; over the sombre hills
beyond, which divided from the great county
of Yorkshire, and across which now poured
the morning sunlight, warm and golden ; away
still on over moor and dale, town and river,
till the sea was reached. He recalled a
certain holiday-time in his exuberant and
energetic youth when he casually met on the
glistening sands between the cliffs and the
gentle summer sea his two old schoolfellows,
John and Harry Raynor, accompanied by
their sister Joanna—tall and handsome, as
Isabel now was—and by Joanna's school-
friend, Mary Weatherly. How he remembered, as though it were yesterday, that his
heart leaped when he set eyes on Joanna, and

he exclaimed confidently to himself : ' That's
the girl that I shall marry ! '   He walked on
with Joanna, on and on over the shining
sands, and let the brothers Raynor have Mary
Weatherly between them.   Mary's position
that day was symptomatic and suggestive of
what was to follow : she was divided between
the two brothers ; she liked both, but she had
to choose one, and she first chose Harry.   But
even then John—as he was in honour bound
to do—did not cease to think of her.   He
still plied her with his attentions and impor-
tunities, and being in some ways—in manners
and speech especially—more attractive than
Harry, he weaned the girl's perplexed affections
from his brother.   The sad and dishonourable
end came when Harry was away accomplish-
ing with herculean energy a task that was
to expedite the time of his marriage ; that
was the season chosen by John to overcome
the last scruples of his brother's affianced

wife. He married her in haste and secrecy, and carried her off to London, where the pair had occasion to repent at leisure. Harry was wounded to the quick, and his life was diverted into a new channel. He went away to do business in India, whence his restlessness and recklessness had driven him to be a traveller of the old kind—explorer and merchant, that is, in one—in the little-known and dangerous States that lie between India and China. He had entered Tibet, when it was thought that death only would be the portion of any stranger who showed his face in that exclusive table-land; and he had almost penetrated the secret of the Lamas, and knew more about Esoteric Buddhism and its Mahatmas and Chelas than any other European. He had escaped from the hands and guards of a ruthless khan of Chinese Tartary, and had crossed without mishap from Calcutta to Tonkin when Upper Burma

and the Shan States were scarcely adventured
upon.   He had spent five-and-twenty years in
that dangerous and unusual kind of life—years
during. which his brother John had disappeared from knowledge in the seething abyss
of London—his wife having died, and his
daughter being surrendered to the care of
his sister, Mrs. Suffield—years during which
Suffield had become a wealthy manufacturer.
Harry Raynor, too, had won wealth—wealth
and fame—and now he had returned to his
own people to end his days, if so be that
his restless soul would permit him to be
so much like other men.

So many things had happened to George
Suffield since he had married Joanna Raynor
—the years had been so filled with business and pleasure, with duties and cares,
private and public—that he was amazed
and perplexed to discover that Uncle Harry
had not forgotten the loss of twenty-five

years ago, that his wound was not yet healed, or that, if it were healed, it was only covered with a cicatrice which throbbed painfully to the slightest touch. He did not consider that probably Uncle Harry's years of travel and adventure were but a long parenthesis of merely bodily and mental experience, and that now when he had returned to his native land he had resumed the feeling of his life where he had dropped it.

Uncle Harry soon returned, fresh and rosy, from his dip in the cold stream, and Suffield, inwardly ejaculating, 'Poor old Harry!' took his arm, and was marched briskly towards the house. In the garden they saw the tall, dark, and stately Isabel walking lovingly with the small, fair, and clinging Euphemia.

'I can't think,' said Suffield, considering his daughter from afar, 'who my girl takes after. I'm big, and so's her mother.'

'Perhaps,' said Uncle Harry, 'she takes after her great-grandmother.'

Suffield looked at him and laughed, regarding the suggestion as a joke, and said, 'On which side?'

'I don't know,' said Uncle Harry seriously, for he had made a study of the small matters of heredity. 'But you often find curious instances of atavism, or harking back to remote ancestors.'

'You may hark back a long while,' said Suffield, ' before they'll speak.'

'You don't seem to understand, George,' said Uncle Harry. 'I mean this kind of thing: I, for instance, am very like, I believe, in appearance and disposition to my great-grandfather, who was as great a rover by sea as I have been by land. As for you, George, I believe you are like nobody but yourself; you are unique; you are, in your own way, the kind of man, like Shakespeare or Milton, that's born once in a thousand years for the admiration and delight of the world.'

'That's a high kind of pedestal you'd like me to mount, Harry,' said Suffield; 'but I'm not such a fool. Seems to me you want some solid food in you to keep you from flights of fancy. I must hurry breakfast up when we get in.'

Tummas answered his summons at the Hall door, and a matron of imperial presence met him on his entrance. She had the front of Juno, an eye kindly but shrewd, and a nose and chin that denoted such firmness of character as might have been suspected to be obstinacy, had the suspicion not been subdued by the soft curves of the mouth. This was Mrs. Suffield.

'Goodness gracious, George!' she exclaimed when she saw him, 'look at your feet. Why didn't you put on your goloshes?'

'Oh, ah; yes,' he said, looking down at

his boots ; ' they are a little damp, Joan.   But I'll take no harm.'

' Damp ! ' exclaimed his wife. ' They're sopping wet ! You must take them off at once !'

' Well, now,' said Suffield, laughing, ' look at Harry's boots.   Hadn't he better take his off too ? '

' Oh, Harry,' said Harry's sister, presenting her cheek to be kissed, ' may do as he likes. A man that would rather sleep on the damp, cold ground than in a dry, warm bed, must take the responsibility of his own feet and of his own health in general.'

' There's for you, Harry ! ' exclaimed Suffield, with a laugh of something like enjoyment. ' That's how I'm always ordered and disposed of ! You'd better come and change your things.'

' Don't be long,' said Mrs. Suffield. ' We are going to have breakfast early : we have a busy day before us.'

CHAPTER III

THE BLACK TULIP AND THE LILY OF THE VALLEY

MEANWHILE, Isabel Raynor and her cousin Euphemia Suffield wandered in the sunny garden. If they were not 'in maiden meditation, fancy free,' as they walked along the gravelled paths with their arms about each other, they at least appeared to be. The flowers were late that year, and Whitsuntide was early. There was not a hint of rosebuds; but the garden was gay with the last of the blooms of spring, especially with beds of tulips, for which Suffield had the love of a Dutchman. Fragrant and beautiful, however, as were the flowers in the freshness of the morning, they seemed but sweet and illustrative notes and comments on the beauty of the two maidens that walked among them. A fanciful young poet, who afterwards saw the young ladies together in other scenes, called them the Black Tulip and the Lily of the Valley. Had he seen them together on that particular morning his floreate fancy would have appeared less forced; for, with the prodigal suggestions of the garden about them, Isabel, in her dark dress and with her rich dark beauty, indeed seemed the human embodiment, express and admirable, of the Black Tulip of Dumas's unfortunate and long-suffering hero—tall and straight, with a full and gorgeous cup; while the fair Euphemia, small and sylph-like, and arrayed in white, looked by contrast with her as the complete realisation of the shy and tender Lily of the Valley blooming in its sheath of green.

The Black Tulip and the Lily of the

Valley were in close personal contact; but their meditations, to judge from their aspect, were wide apart. Isabel, moderating her naturally stately gait to Euphemia's convenience, paced along with a serious, not to say sad, countenance; for she felt that her uncle Harry, to whose coming she had looked forward with so lively an interest, if he did not absolutely dislike her, held his liking in abeyance, as if she were primarily under suspicion—and that she both resented and failed to understand. Her cousin, on the contrary, stepped as to a measure, and let her bright eyes rove carelessly round, now and again whistling excellent imitations of the episodical and sleepy notes of the garden birds, drowsy after their early debauch of song.

'Oh, I do love to be up early in the summer-time!' exclaimed Euphemia, in her happy carelessness failing to remark her cousin's serious abstraction. 'Don't *you*, Isabel?—don't *you*?'

'I do, my dear,' answered Isabel, smiling on her. ' I like to be up early all the year round. It's so pleasant, as Sir Walter Scott used to say, to break the neck of the day's work before breakfast.'

'How do you know Sir Walter Scott used to say that?' asked Euphemia, with a touch of childlike pique and wonder on her face.

'How do I know? I've read it, of course, my dear,' said Isabel, with a look of wonder in her turn.

'What a lot of things you seem to read, Isabel! You always make me feel like a goose; when you're not here, I rather fancy myself as a clever sort of person.'

'My dear Phemy!' exclaimed Isabel, 'it's not right of me to make you feel like a goose, because you are not a goose at all, but a very bright, dear, clever little song-bird!'

'Oh, it's nice of you to say that, Bell!' said Phemy, hugging her cousin's arm. 'I like it, you know, though I don't believe it's true.'

'It is true, indeed, my dear,' said Isabel; 'and I shall blame myself very much if anything I may say should somehow make you think poorly of yourself. Forgive me, dear. It is only my schoolmistress way, which I am afraid I can't very easily get out of, to quote books I've read and to name authors I happen to be interested in. I'll try not to do it, my. dear.'

'I wish you were not a schoolmistress, Bell.'

'What would you have me be? A mill-girl, or a milliner, or a telegraphist?'

'Bell! you know well enough it is not necessary that you should be anything but a lady.'

'Merely to be a lady, dear,' said Isabel,

' is not an occupation by which you can make a hundred and fifty pounds a year; and to be a schoolmistress is.'

'You know what I mean, Bell,' said Euphemia. 'Father always says he has more for us all than he knows what to do with. Why don't you stay with us altogether? I daresay father would give you a hundred and fifty a year for yourself.'

'My dear Phemy, I know Uncle George is the best and kindest and most generous man in the world. He is too good, but—— Well, the fact is I can't endure to be idle, and I like to earn my hundred and fifty for myself in my own way.'

'I can't understand,' said Phemy, 'why you want to be so independent. It's not like a girl at all,' she added, while she blankly felt and vaguely resented that Isabel was stronger, cleverer, more resolute than a woman had any right to be. It was absurd

—and in a sense improper—in a woman to strive to provide herself with those things which fathers (and husbands) were expressly created to find for her. 'I suppose, then, Bell, you wouldn't marry a man with money unless you had money too?'

'I should prefer to have some money of my own,' answered Isabel, as if she were delivering an opinion which she had seriously pondered. 'But I think that "in that connection," as the Americans say, it would not matter much if I had money or my husband had money, or we both had nothing but hands and heads to provide a living. Marriage, you see, is like no other relationship; it is— or it should be, I think—not the joining of two persons together, but the bringing together of the two parts of one complete person.'

'Like a hook and an eye, I suppose?' said Euphemia.

'If you like to put it like that, my dear,' answered Isabel; and then she continued the serious exposition of her view of marriage. 'So, you see, what the one has belongs to both, and what the one wants the other makes up. There can be no question of mine or thine, of different interests, if they are properly matched—that is, I suppose,' she added half-musingly, 'if they truly and un- reservedly love each other.'

'What a queer girl you are, Isabel!' ex- claimed Euphemia.

'Am I? Perhaps I am,' said Isabel with resignation.

'How you can think of all these awfully wise things, I can't make out!'

'I can't help thinking of "things," as you call them, when I'm alone.'

'Well,' said Euphemia, returning in triumph to the point of conviction she had at first wished to make, ' that's what I tell you : you've no business to be alone.   Father always says it's an absurd shame that a clever, handsome girl like you should not get married. Tell me now, Bell dear, just between our two selves, why you won't accept George?'

'Really, Phemy dear, that is a plain question !'

'Don't you think him nice?   Don't you like him?' urged Phemy.

'I like him very much ; but——'

'Do you like any one else better?' pursued Phemy.

'That's not the question, my dear,' said Isabel, evading the point with a light laugh. 'To think,' she exclaimed with another laugh, 'that all my serious lecture about marriage has been thrown away! Don't you understand, my dear, that in my view a girl must not only like a man, but understand and admire him, and sympathise with his ambitions very much, to be ready to spend all her life with him? I couldn't marry George —though it's impertinent to say that, since he has never asked me—but I couldn't marry him, because I don't think I could spend all my life with him.'

'But,' said Phemy, 'don't you think you could have an affection for a man you didn't admire in those other ways?'

'Oh, affection!' said Isabel; 'that's another thing. But I think I give all my affection to my family—to uncle and aunt, and you and George. You may have affection for a person you wouldn't care to marry.'

'George hasn't asked you yet, Bell,' said Euphemia, with a clear intention in her tone, 'but depend upon it he will ask you.'

'You don't mean you will tell him?' exclaimed Isabel in a hot flush of maidenly alarm. 'If you tell him, Phemy, what I have said to you in confidence, I will never forgive you!'

'I won't say anything to him about it, my dear' said Phemy. 'Don't be so afraid. But do tell me one thing more: what kind of man do you think you could love very, very much?'

Isabel, however, evidently thought she had said enough in confidence; for she answered lightly: 'I don't think I could ever love a man that was not at least twenty years older than myself; I couldn't respect a younger man.'

'Now, you're not serious,' said Euphemia with a pout; 'and I won't tell you the kind of man I could love very, very much.'

'Oh, do tell me that, please, Phemy dear,' said Isabel, relieved and gratified that confidence was now to be diverted to the other side.

'Well,' said Euphemia, hugging still closer her cousin's arm, 'the man I would love very much must be like my dear father. He may be as old as he likes——'

'What?' said Isabel. 'Seventy or eighty?'

'No; not quite so old as that. I think thirty will do. He needn't be very good-looking—I don't think I care for good-looking men: they're so much taken up with themselves and their hair and moustaches—but he must be very good and very kind and very generous. But there's the breakfast bell; we mustn't keep mother waiting. I'll tell you some other time.'

CHAPTER IV

THE TAME PHILOSOPHER

WHEN they entered the breakfast-room, the household was already assembled for morning prayers, and the master of the house sat in his place at the table with the prayer-book before him, and the unopened letter-bag and the uncut morning paper ready to his hand. Isabel and her cousin dropped silently into vacant seats by the door, and the function went on, Isabel, it must be confessed, feeling and showing considerable pre-occupation : she was familiar with that kind of thing twice a day at school. The prayers were decorously and feelingly read, while Tummas, who was a privileged client of the house, and who had been brought up in the Methodist communion, interjected at every pause of the master a fervent 'Amen!' and then the men-servants and maid-servants trooped out with a cheerful countenance to the day's duties and relaxations. Then also Mr. Suffield turned with alacrity to the letter-bag, to which he and his wife alone possessed a key. He opened it while the family took their places at table, and Tummas brought in the hot dishes.

'Here's two for you, mother,' said Suffield, dealing out the letters; 'three for you, George—and one o' them in a lady's hand: that won't do, lad; three, four, five, six— bless me!—seven, eight for " H. Raynor, Esq., C.M.G.!" That must be you, Harry; and most o' them directed and redirected. Ah, Isabel, my lass, and here's one solitary epistle for you. H'm! seems to me I ought to know the fist. Redirected twice over. Well, there you are.'

Isabel took her letter and opened it with misgiving. The first words she read blanched her face to a deathly shade, and almost made her faint with grief, pain, and apprehension. But no one noticed her emotion—except George, who always kept an interested eye on her—because of the entrance of a guest, and Isabel devoured part of her letter unquestioned.

Mr. Suffield kept open house and a lavish table without ostentation; for it is altogether a mistake to suppose that only those who have inherited landed estates and personalty running to five or six figures have the art of frank and free hospitality. That is really not an art at all, but an instinct, humane and hearty; and the costermonger may in his degree possess it as much as, if not more than, the duke. Mr. Suffield's nature was lordly, if not ducal; and the amount he disbursed in casual largess, as well as in regular beneficence and undemonstrative hospitality, would have impoverished many a man of considerable means. Many and various were the 'friends' who dropped in at meal-times when the master was known to be at home, but of all, none was more constant in his friendly habit than the present visitor, Mr. Ebenezer M'Fie. He seldom came when Mr. Suffield was away—for he seemed to know that he was not greatly admired or beloved by the mistress of the house—but when Suffield was at home he came regularly to breakfast. He was a dry and somewhat toothless little Scotsman, who had failed as schoolmaster and as editor, and who now lived—it was suspected, but scarcely known—on certain meagre earnings as a teacher and preacher and on occasional 'loans'—or, more properly, gifts—from his generous friend Suffield. He was not a very estimable person; but Suffield delighted in him—in his learning and his eloquence. Mrs. Suffield unkindly called him 'George's tame philosopher,' and not infrequently hinted that the sole reason of her husband's belief in the tame philosopher's wisdom was that he was the only one besides himself whom he had ever heard talk; her inveterate opinion being that her husband monopolised usually the conversation of the house. The philosopher's style of speech seemed to be modelled on the writings of the late Thomas Carlyle; it was English—of a heavy and involved kind—but it was uttered with so abominable an accent that it was unintelligible to most people. Mr. Suffield had given attention to it, and therefore seemed to understand it; but his son, who had not patience to quarry a meaning out of the rugged and barbarous eloquence of the philosopher, did not scruple at times to call him 'an old ass.'

'George Suffield,' exclaimed the philosopher now, fervently shaking hands with his host, 'I'm glad to see ye again, hale and hearty, out o' that welter o' humanity, that roaring loom o' Time they call London.'

'I'm not here for long, though, Eben,' said Suffield, returning his pressure.

'Yet a little while—I know, man. But ye may abide among your own people longer than ye at the present thoughtless fleeting moment intend. Ye *may*. I *hope* ye may. The domain of the Possible, man, is immeasurably spacious; there are no limits to the realm of Hope.'

'Just so, Eben,' said Suffield, 'but——'

'Fiddle-de-dee, my dear,' said his wife. 'The sausages are getting cold; will you help them? I'm much as usual, thank you, Mr. M'Fie,' said she in answer to the philosopher's polite inquiry concerning her well-being. 'Will you sit here? This is my brother, Mr. Harry Raynor; the others you know.

Isabel, dear, that's a steak-and-kidney pie before you. You don't look well, my dear; you and Phemy have been out too early.'

'I'm very well, thank you, aunt,' answered Isabel, recovering herself with an effort: her letter she had already put in her pocket—she feared to finish reading it then.

George watched her with perturbed spirit and jealous eye: from whom, he asked himself, could have come the letter which had caused her such lively emotion, and which she had crammed away unread?—from whom but from a lover? And yet her emotion did not seem to be of a pleasant kind. Could it be that the lover was ill? In order to hide his perturbation and to refrain from conversation, George opened out the 'Lancashire Gazette.' He found and began to read the notice of the play which he had seen the night before, and which had been discussed on his father's return. He was quickly interested. He usually affected to despise all except metropolitan journalism, but here was vigorous and fearless writing which he was compelled to respect and admire. He could not contain his interest.

'By jingo!' he exclaimed, 'here's Alan Ainsworth going it like one o'clock!'

'"Going it like one o'clock,"' said the philosopher, pausing with a bit of toast near his mouth, 'is a strange phrase of the vulgar tongue, and to the undiscerning eye appears absurd and meaningless. It would be curious to inquire concerning its origin—whence and how—by what association, concatenation, or linking of ideas, it comes to be used to express the extremity of speed, vigour, or abandonment.'

That was properly regarded but as a reflective parenthesis that did not demand discussion. Suffield took polite note of it, however.

'Yes; just so, Eben,' said he; and then

turned to his son with lively concern, and asked: 'Pitching into the play, is he? It's sure to be well done. Read it out, lad.'

Isabel, for her part, welcomed this request of her uncle: it would keep curious eyes and questions from herself—she was conscious of appearing pale and disturbed—it would spare her the necessity of making and sharing in conversation; and the interest of the matter might turn her mind a little from the trouble that had seized it. George read, nothing loth, while his father interjected 'H'ms' and 'Ha's' of acceptation or approval, and the philosopher listened with his hand to his ear and with the air of a man who had been in his time a schoolmaster and an editor, and withal a critic. The article was what is commonly called 'a slating' of both play and players; and the 'slating' was very vigorously done, spite of the fact that concerning both players and play London was supposed to be very enthusiastic. 'A noble tragedy,' declared the critic, 'which was altogether unsuited to stage representation, has been laid sacrilegious hands on by the play-wright and the play-actor, and the result is an indifferent melodrama, badly acted;' with much more, general and particular, to the same effect. Finally he said: 'Of course the play has been hailed in London as a triumph of stage management and acting; but it is in reality a triumph of pedantry, dulness, and incapacity.'

'What do you think of that?' cried Suffield in triumph, when the reading was finished. 'That's just what you were trying to say last night, I suppose, Isabel?'

'Just what I was *trying* to say, uncle?' said Isabel with a smile.

'Yes,' said the philosopher, looking round, perking himself, and clearly demanding the attention of the table; 'the young man writes with great promise—great promise indeed.'

'Mr. Ainsworth,' said young George, 'if I understand him at all, would hope there is performance as well as promise.'

'No doubt, sir; no doubt, my young friend,' said the philosopher. Then, eluding the point presented, he continued: 'He is right. We are the slaves of Rumour. We accept alike the reputation of book or man——'

'Or play,' suggested George.

'Or play,' accepted the philosopher.

'Or play-actor,' suggested George, pleased with his success.

'Or play-actor, sir,' again accepted the philosopher. 'We accept their reputation, if it be made in London, let us say——'

'Or made in Germany,' again suggested George.

'—— because,' continued the philosopher, without taking account this time of the interruption, 'we are ourselves incompetent to distinguish between the estimate of ignorant exaggeration and that of the authentic insight of the few who know what they say and say only what they know.'

'You're eating no breakfast, Mr. M'Fie,' said Mrs. Suffield. 'George, my dear, see that Mr. M'Fie has something;' whereupon Suffield recommended the dish before him.

'Ah,' said the philosopher, 'I believe that in the great metropolis they call these little things saveloys?'

'Sausages, sir; these are sausages,' said young George. 'Saveloys are, I understand, a very inferior and vulgar kind of sausage.'

'Mixed originally, I think the dictionaries say,' Isabel was tempted to remark, 'with brains—as Sir Joshua Reynolds said his colours were.' Then, remembering her promise in the garden to Euphemia, she said aside to her: 'I beg your pardon, dear.'

'Now,' said the philosopher, shaking him-

self up as if he were a bottle of medicine, ' I
call that very good ; really witty, and of
the true Attic flavour.   I do.'

'Oh yes, Isabel's a smart girl,' observed
Suffield genially ; then, with his kindly eye
more particularly on his brother-in-law, he
insisted : ' I say, Isabel's a clever girl.'

' No doubt,' said Uncle Harry, while he
shrewdly considered his niece.

' Please, uncle,' said Isabel, blushing with
confusion, and appealing to Suffield in a low
voice, ' don't—don't make me ashamed of
myself ! '

' No need, my lass,' said Suffield aloud, ' to
be ashamed of yourself ! '

But Isabel thought there was, especially
with Uncle Harry's shrewd eye, which she
felt to be cold and critical, fixed on her.   She
lapsed into a painful silence, on the sudden
suspicion that she must appear a very forward
and conceited young woman.   But why did

Uncle Harry—her father's own brother—regard her so? Why did he look at her, not only without affection or tenderness, but, it seemed to her, with absolute aversion? Did she strike him as being so disagreeable a creature, either in character or in appearance, or in both?

'But,' said the philosopher, seizing the opportunity of the pause, 'to return to the interesting subject we were discussing. I said a few minutes ago that we are the slaves of Rumour. About this play now: we either accept the opinion of the great Babylon, borne on the wings of the newspapers, or we accept this young man's opinion.'

'*I* don't,' said young George promptly.

'My dear young sir,' said the philosopher, 'I question that. You think that you don't. To all but a few'—and there was a clear hint in his eye and his manner that he considered himself one of the few—'current report is irrefutable evidence. To see with our own eyes—to hear with our own ears——'

'Goodness me!' exclaimed Mrs. Suffield impatiently; 'whose ears should I hear with if not with my own?'

'Ah, my dear lady,' crackled on the philosopher, now enjoying himself immensely, ' this commonly thought easiest of all things is of things hard to be done one of the hardest—nay, the hardest of all.' And so on, and so on, he continued, becoming more and more intoxicated with the sound of his own voice and swollen with the volume of his own verbosity.

And his audience seemed to listen with attention and interest. The excellent Suffield, however, was the only person who toiled after him through his obscure and sounding platitudes, in the single-minded hope of carrying away some wisdom. All the others were more or less occupied with things of livelier and more intimate concern. Mrs. Suffield was thinking over her arrangements for the day—and at the same time giving a ray of attention to her niece, who looked very much less than her usual self that morning; George was still considering, half in pity, half in jealousy, his cousin's preoccupation and depression; Euphemia was chilled and saddened because, evidently, Isabel cherished a feeling for some one of which she had refused to let her know; Uncle Harry was wondering whether Isabel added to her faults of self-consciousness and conceit that of sulkiness; and Isabel herself was thinking of that letter which was burning her pocket, and resenting—as unkindly and undeserved—the cold and critical regard under which Uncle Harry was keeping her. The notable thing was that to all save to the philosopher and his simple-minded patron and pupil, and to Isabel herself, the real centre of interest was Isabel.

'Well, now, my dear,' said Mrs. Suffield at length to her husband, thrusting into a pause in the philosopher's discourse, 'we have a great many things to do to-day, and we haven't yet begun to do any of them. The girls and I must see to things,' continued she, rising. 'George, my dear, will you ring the bell?—If you, my dear,' said she again to her husband, 'want to discuss the affairs of the universe with Mr. M‘Fie, you'd better take him into the garden.'

'My dear lady,' said the philosopher, 'I and your husband have had our say, I think.' (As matter of fact, Suffield had said nothing but 'H'm!' or 'Ye-es' now and then.)

The philosopher rose then and straggled out through the open French window into the garden. Suffield was politely following him, when Uncle Harry laid his hand on his arm.

'Who,' he asked, 'is your Mentor, George?'

'I don't know about Mentor,' answered Suffield, ' but he is a curious, clever creature.'

' Strong in the wind, but weak in the legs, I should think, George,' said Uncle Harry.

'I shall be back to you in a minute or two, aunt,' said Isabel; and she fled to her room and locked herself in to read her letter.

CHAPTER V

ISABEL'S LETTER

ISABEL first considered again the envelope of her letter. It had been, as her uncle Suffield said, redirected twice. It had first gone to the Ladies' College where she taught; thence it had been sent to her lodgings; whence it had been forwarded to her at her uncle's. The significance of these directions and the poverty of the paper on which they were written having been duly pondered, she opened the letter itself. She had seen the handwriting only twice in her life before, and yet it ought to have been familiar to her eyes, for it was her father's. The following is the curious epistle which Isabel read, and which the acute reader will find full of suggestion :

My DR CHILD,—you w^l wonder exceed^{g}ly th^t you sh^d hear again fr y^r poor, unfort^{te} father. I h wander^d t round earth ov^r (tho', as a teacher o youth, you are aware th^t t earth is not a perfect sphere, but flatten^d at t ends o t axis like an orange) ' fr China to Peru ' (*vide* any standrd book o quota^{ns}) since last I h^d t parent^l del^t o writ^g to you. It w^d achieve no desir^{ble} end to relate to you in det^l my wander^{gs} and adventures, my gains (insignific^t) and my losses (considera^{ble}), my br^t-wing^d hope and my dull-ey^{ed} despair. T fact, howev^r, th^t my pres^t address f correspond^{ce} is Mrs. Ackland Snow, Tobacconist, Nelson Street, New North Road, N.,—wh, as you may be aware, is contigu^s to ' Merrie Islingt^n,'—must speak to you w an eloqu^{ce} all its own. Aft^r these diverse experi^{ces} (in t

main adverse) I am again a miser^(ble) denizen o
our modern Babylon. Moreov^(r) in t humble
dwell^(g) w^(re) I am at pres^(t) domicil^(d) I am detain^(d) as
a kind o person^(l) pledge f a debt o two-twelve-
six. I am permitt^(d) to go out only to call f lett^(rs)
or to post them, and th^(t) under t vigil^(t) surveill^(ce)
o my landlady's son, a sharp London boy who
'has no little handkerchf'—you know t
quot^(n). I expect noth^(g) as t result o this
communic^(n), as I deserve noth^(g);—yet if we all
h^(d) our deserts—? I h t unshak^(n) convic^(n),
howev^(r), th^(t) there still resides in y^(r) bosom
some filial regard to^(rds) him who, tho' unworthy o t name, cannot but subscribe hims^(f)
—y^(r) father,

JOHN RAYNOR.

Two or three things were obviously remarkable about this letter: it was written on
a half-sheet of paper, which was of as poor
quality as that of the envelope; it contained

contractions in spelling which suggested that the writer either had or had had experience of some walk in journalism; and it expressed sentiments and made statements which very plainly implied that John Raynor was a somewhat shady and shifty person.

Isabel stood by her dressing-table in the light of the window, and looked meditatively forth into the sunlit garden while she mechanically folded and folded again the flimsy paper in her hand till it was of the appearance of a pipelight. This was the third letter she had received from her father, and all three were in the same strain. The first came to her four years before, when she was first appointed teacher in the Ladies' College, and she had replied to it with money, and the request that her father would let her see him. That, however, he refused to do; but he begged for more money to go to America and to take up a ' literary appointment' which had been offered him : and that was his second letter. She had answered it as he had desired, with considerable difficulty, and had heard no more until now. The four years which had passed since her father had gone to America had widened considerably not only her knowledge of books, but her understanding also of men and women, so that this third letter appealed as to a different person, and provoked doubts and apprehensions altogether new. The father who thus wrote to her she had not seen since she was five years old, when her mother had died and her aunt had taken charge of her. She had, therefore, but a dim recollection of him—a dull child would probably have had no recollection at all—but such recollection as she had, which had been wakened and clarified by the sight of her uncle, was bewildered by the letter. Her father, as she now recalled him, was much taller than her uncle—but that, she admitted to herself, might be only in the view of a child, to whom all grown-up people seem tall —but in other ways he was like her uncle; he was reticent and serious, and seemed severe. He was therefore scarcely the person—it now occurred to her—to write such an epistle as that she now held between her fingers, or as those she had received four years before. Could it be, she asked herself suddenly, that she had been imposed upon by this person, whom she had believed to be her father because he had so represented himself, and because he had recalled certain family matters which she had thought only her father could know? She might, she considered, have her doubt set at rest by showing the letter to either of her uncles and saying, ' Tell me if this be my father's hand or no ! ' but then she remembered that her uncle George had remarked when he handed her the

letter, that he ought to know 'the fist'—
as if he dimly recognised it—and she shrank
from making known, even to her uncles, her
father's condition, if this person who had
written as her father were her father indeed.

She still hoped he was; for when her
father—or this person who was not her
father—had first written to her, she had had
a waking dream of the kind that was sure
to invade a good and generous girl. She
had gathered vaguely, and at intervals, during her schooltime, when she spent her holi-
days at her uncle's, that her father, if he was
not dead, was leading a life of so disreputable
a sort that his existence must be ignored.
She had not ventured to ask either her aunt
or her uncle what his offences were; but her
aunt was so severe and even unjust to her
on occasion, that she concluded her father's
fault must be neither unforgivable nor
irremediable. When, therefore, he put him-

self in communication with her, her heart leaped forth to help and save him. Her impulse was not so much that of a daughter as that of a mother.

Men are slow to recognise—and slower to believe—that the earliest and the most potent affection of a good girl of strong character is maternal. She first expends it upon her dolls, and her younger brothers and sisters—when she has them—and then she lavishes it upon her lover, who is somewhat bewildered by this divine mixture of feeling for himself, until he is husband and father, when the new feeling in his own breast teaches him to understand hers. Isabel's circumstances had dammed up the flow of this kind of affection. She had been too clever in her girlhood, and too much occupied with books and duties, to be seriously concerned about dolls, and neither her cousins nor her fellow pupils at school had needed her attentions. It was therefore with all the more overwhelming volume that this maternal feeling rushed towards her father when he made himself known. He had pushed it back again by his refusal to see her and by his flight to America; but again it was seeking vent, now that he was returned and was within reach—if it was indeed he who had written to her. She passionately hoped that it might be he.

As she considered and hoped, she resolved what she would do; for Nature and training had conspired to make her a person of quick decision. She would send some money at once, with a promise to send more in a few days—when, that is, she would be in London, could observe and discover for herself the person who would call for it. She would stop him and speak to him. If he were not her father, then all would be at an end; but if he were, then—oh, then!—with what passionate joy would she take him to her heart to tend and comfort him, to strengthen and restore him. It never occurred to her to doubt whether her father, if found, would be worth such wealth of love; for her feeling was of the serene quality of divine mercy, which regards no sinner as beyond hope of redemption.

A tap sounded at her door, and a voice—Euphemia's—said : 'Bell, dear, will you be long ? Mother wants us to go into town.'

There at once was presented Isabel's desired opportunity. 'I'll put my things on and be down in a moment,' answered she.

When she descended—with her purse and her letter in her pocket—she found that her aunt and her cousin had gone into the regions of the kitchen. Thither she followed them, and came upon both at the back-door of the mansion. Her aunt was there—a person to behold and consider. The front of her stately figure was arrayed in a large linen

apron with a bib, and she was superintending
the unloading of a baker's van piled with
buns for the children's Whitsuntide ' treat ' in
the park that day. She had torn open one of
the buns, to judge if they were well-baked
and white within, and to ascertain that they
were not too meagrely supplied with currants.
She stood eating a morsel and holding the
fragments in her hand, while she counted
with the baker the fourteen to the dozen
which he threw into great baskets waiting
to receive them. And Isabel, as she beheld
and considered, wondered for the first time
whether the prosperity of the house of
Suffield was mainly due to the husband or
to the wife.

That duty accomplished, her aunt turned
to her with a keen but not unkindly look—
a look, indeed, which seemed to say : ' There's
something wrong ; I wish we two understood
each other better.' What she actually did

say was: ' You're not looking quite yourself, Bell.　No bad news, I hope?'

' No, aunt,' answered Isabel.　' It's nothing to speak of.　It's only a letter that has been forwarded to me from London.'

' Of course,' said her aunt, somewhat drily, with the clear significance of ' I knew *that.*'　But she added: ' I only hoped you had nothing to really worry· you.　I don't want to pry into your private concerns.'

' I have no private concerns of any consequence, aunt,' she said with a blush.

' Well,' said her aunt, dismissing the matter, ' I want you and Phemy to go into town—the horses are being put into the landau—and order these things '—producing a list from her pocket—' at our drapers', Wigmore and Kendal.　You will see the kind of things they have in stock.　You know what I like; and if you see they haven't got the proper things, tell them to get them somewhere else, or to get them made. When all the order is ready, tell them the things are to be sent to that address a week hence—Rutland Gate, London, W.'

'Oh, mother!' exclaimed Euphemia, clasping her hands in ecstasy, 'are we really going to London then for the season?'

'Yes, my dear,' said her mother, looking on her with indulgent eye, 'we are going to London. Your father has taken the house and most of the furniture over from the Earl of Padiham.'

'What!' exclaimed Euphemia. 'The Earl of Padiham that lives out here on the moors?'

'To be sure, my dear,' said her mother, with a laugh; 'you don't suppose the peerage can contain two Earls of Padiham?'

'What! Isn't it big enough to hold two, mother?'

'Don't be a goose!' said Mrs. Suffield with

a touch of severity; for she suspected her daughter was inclined to jibe, and she caught a twinkle of amusement passing from her niece's eye. 'Now make haste, both of you. The carriage is waiting, I've no doubt.'

'But,' asked her daughter, 'aren't you going to tell me all about our going to London?'

'Tell you all about it! There's time enough for that before we go. One thing at a time. Be off now, and do your business.' They were hurrying away when she called after them: 'You might call at the office of the "Gazette" on your way back, both of you, and bring Mr. Ainsworth along; he is usually there, I think, just before lunch-time, and he's capital at amusing children— almost as good as yourself, Bell.'

Isabel accepted the suggestion with silence. She understood completely the intention of her aunt. She had perceived before to-day that her aunt was ever ready to bring Alan Ainsworth and herself together, a readiness which, while partly due, doubtless, to the liking her aunt had for the young journalist, was much more due, Isabel believed, to the fact that Mrs. Suffield had a loftier ambition for her son than he had for himself.

CHAPTER VI

ALAN AINSWORTH

THE editorial sanctum of a leading provincial newspaper of these days is almost as unapproachable by the vulgar as that of the 'Times' itself. It may be set in quite as imposing a building, and may be the centre of almost as great a spider's web of political 'influence,' 'special' correspondence, and news 'agency' as the journal that boasts the largest circulation in the world: that may be taken for granted without further insistence.

The terra-cotta palace inhabited by the 'Lancashire Gazette' is reckoned an ornament of one of the finest and busiest streets of the city which claims to be the heart and soul of the County Palatine ; and the editor's room is the finest, though not the largest, of all the rooms in that palace.

While Isabel and her cousin were busy with their shopping, about that mid-day hour when the growing young men in the office became wistfully interested in the impassive face of the office clock, a somewhat stoutish and florid gentleman stood on the hearthrug of the editorial room in the attitude which none but its master would have ventured to adopt. His hands were behind him, and his coat-tails were parted, though the grate was empty, and he stood squarely and solidly, bearing a little on his toes as he measured out his utterances, and marking the emphasis of his words with that slight motion of the head which is all the reserved and weighty Englishman permits himself by way of gesture. This was Frederick Smith, the famous chief of the ' Lancashire Gazette.' He was an admirable example of the kind of person ticketed by Carlyle as 'Able Editor,' and he was addressing no casual caller, for no such common mortal would be admitted to his presence. Before him paced irregularly to and fro, making occasional pauses for speech, a tall, spare, and broad-shouldered young man, excited and flushed.

'I think, sir,' said the young man, when they had been talking thus for some time, 'that if a critic must not express his honest convictions, you might as well get a reporter to do his work.'

'You are a young man, Mr. Ainsworth,' said the able editor, 'and I say this for your good : it is part of the intolerance of youth to be always wishing to utter its " honest con-victions," and it is part of the regret of maturer years to know that the " honest con-victions " of youth have been only impatient prejudices. That you will discover before you are as old as I am, and I certainly must ask you in the meantime to tone down the severity of your dramatic notices.'

' If I cannot say, sir,' said Ainsworth, ' what I honestly think and feel about a performance, I had rather not do the theatres at all.'

' Very well, Mr. Ainsworth,' said the editor ; ' that is a point for yourself alone to decide, though I would advise you not to be rash. I like your work ; in other respects it suits me completely, and I should be sorry to lose it. Think it over.'

And the able editor took his right hand from behind him, and held it out for Ainsworth to shake. Ainsworth grasped it, dropped it, and went.

For an apparently impetuous man, Ainsworth descended the stairs soberly and slowly. On the next landing he encountered a fellow-member of the staff of the ' Gazette,' a dapper young gentleman, who was reputed the most slashing and redoubtable political writer in the Palatinate. Ainsworth nodded to him, and was about to pass on, when the dapper young man stopped and spoke. ' Capital notice that of yours this morning,' said he, ' of the theatre last night. Splendid bit of criticism—straight and clear.'

' I'm glad you like it,' said Ainsworth.

' Yes; I was glad to see it. The play and the players have been too much cockered up by the London papers, and it's an agreeable change to find a critic in the provinces giving them a slating. How does the chief like it? ' he asked with a thin, sly smile.

' The chief,' answered Ainsworth, with reserve, ' cannot be said to be in love with it.'

' I thought not. Never mind. Bye-bye.'

And the two went their several ways— Ainsworth down into the street, and the dapper young gentleman up into the chief's presence.

When Ainsworth had left the building, he stood a moment in hesitation, and then turned down a side street as a man resolved upon a certain course. He entered the restaurant where it was his habit to lunch ; but, since it was not quite his time for luncheon, and since he felt no pressing demand of hunger—his blood was too much determined to his head for that—he merely stood at the bar to eat a hurried biscuit and drink a glass of soda-and-milk. It was too early for any of his fellow-journalists and acquaintances to be about, and of that he was glad ; for he knew that he must look rather glum and preoccupied, and that if his friends saw him so, he would be beset with worrying questions or gibes. His modest biscuit being consumed, he sallied forth and returned into the main street.

He felt the absolute necessity of doing something: his intense excitement was as the rapid generation of steam, impelling him to locomotion. He must go somewhere; he must walk—walk—to revolve and grind away the grave annoyance and anxiety that troubled him. Where should he go? The town would not do: the pavements were crowded, and the thought of dodging and jostling other foot-passengers was painful to him. While he thus considered, he saw a shining open carriage and pair draw up at the kerb a little way ahead of him. He had a keen eye, and he recognised at once the occupants of the carriage—a regal-looking dark beauty and a fairylike fair one, both young, and both arrayed in light summer raiment. They were the daughter and the niece of the excellent Suffield. The tall and stately lady —the niece—descended from the carriage, while the men hurrying by on the pavement

cast over their shoulders admiring glances,
which Ainsworth resented on her behalf.
She stepped into a post-office, over against
which the carriage had stopped, and Ainsworth turned away, that he might not be
recognised by the other lady, and jumped
upon a passing omnibus.

The encounter avoided, he began to think
he was a fool for his pains. Why had he
shunned a meeting with these ladies, the one
of whom he admired as the best read, the
most intelligent, and the most beautiful
woman he had ever known? Why, except
that the trouble which was worrying him
drew him away from contact and from speech
with friend or acquaintance. The sight of
them, however, made him think of his good
friend Suffield, and the thought of him
suggested a walk in the varied and extensive
Holdsworth Park. He had a problem and a
corollary to solve, and he resolved on a

solitary walk to solve them. The omnibus on which he was riding passed the necessary railway station; so there he descended from the knife-board, and entered and took a ticket for Holdsworth.

CHAPTER VII

HOW AINSWORTH SOLVED HIS PROBLEM

WHEN he was on the platform among a crowd of people, he began to wonder whether the days of the week, as well as he, had gone wrong; by the calendar it should be Wednesday, and yet the show of the platform was as that of Saturday. When he entered the train—he travelled third class, as every intelligent, humane, and self-respecting young man should travel—and observed that he was in the midst of those who were plainly holiday-makers, he was certain the times must be out of joint. Then, suddenly, he remembered it was Whitsuntide; and that explained all. For Whitsuntide is the great

Feast—as it were, the Feast of Tabernacles—
—of Lancashire. In the south, men forget
that it is Whitsuntide after Tuesday; but in
Lancashire it is Whitsuntide from Sunday to
Sunday. Then manufactures, mining, and
handicrafts are mostly idle for a week; then
the voice of the cornet and the fife are heard
in the land; and then the whole population
'wallers'—like Tom Sawyer—'in Sunday
schools,' Sunday-school treats, and Sunday-
school processions.

All these manners and customs of Whitsuntide Ainsworth was well enough acquainted
with, but he had forgotten it was Whitsuntide. Now that he remembered, he was struck
with its significance. Were it not that he
was being whirled to Holdsworth as fast as the
Lancashire and Yorkshire Railway Company
could carry him, he would have stayed in
town; for he was sure that Holdsworth Park
would be overrun by the gay and free young

Sunday scholars. But he must go on; and he comforted himself with the thought that, at the worst, Holdsworth Park was large enough to afford some seclusion, even after the Sunday scholars had all the elbow-room they wanted.

At Holdsworth not many passengers left the train. They went their several ways, and he alone went on to Holdsworth Park. In the lane leading towards the village he witnessed a scene which reminded him of a similar one in Charlotte Brontë's 'Shirley,' a scene which it would be impossible to see enacted out of our dear, delightful, absurd, but good-humoured England. From opposite directions came with brazen bands and flaunting banners the Sunday-school processions of church and chapel; and Ainsworth mounted the bank to witness the encounter, for the lane 'was not wide enough to permit each to pass the other freely. On they came with clergyman and pastor at their head, like captains of their troops, and with school teachers distributed along their flanks like sergeants and corporals. When they met, however, the one did not pass triumphantly through the other, as in 'Shirley,' but each halted. The captain of each troop made a sign for silence to his band; he then approached his *vis-à-vis* with his hat off and shook hands with him, and after that gave the word for the band to strike up again— this time the same sacred tune. The bands played the tune through together, the troops facing each other as much as was possible, while some of the non-commissioned and private on either side looked not too well pleased with the situation. Ainsworth, however, was delighted; if the scene was a trifle absurd, it was friendly and humane; and when, the music in common being played, the two troops filed past each other as best they could, he said to himself: ' Behold, how good and how pleasant it is for brethren to dwell together in unity!   But, if I am not mistaken, the real cause of this display of good feeling is that very kindly gentleman, George Suffield. It is impossible for both parson and pastor to be friendly with him—as I am sure they must be—and not to be friendly with each other.   So shines a good man in a naughty world.'

Thus thinking of the admirable Suffield, and all his humane and generous ways, he wandered on into the tidy, trim village and forgot for the time his own anxiety.   The village seemed deserted of all save a few of the very oldest and the very youngest of its population.   Here and there a gaffer or a gammer sat on a doorstep or on a stool against the wall, blinking and basking in the sun, and holding in a striving youngster with a tether of web selvedge and the impassiveness of Fate. Here and there a cat lay on a window-sill, limp with heat, and looking like a dish-clout flung out to dry ; and here and there a dog spread himself at ease in the warm dust of the road, as if he well knew there was no danger to be apprehended from passing carts or other vehicles that day. Through this peaceful scene Ainsworth passed, knowing well its meaning : that all the active population were gone to disport and to feast in Holdsworth Park.

He continued on his way till he reached the lake or dam. He walked to a spot on its bank where grew some alders and threw himself on the turf that sprang soft and green in their shade. Ducks and swans swam towards him in expectation of crumbs ; but he had none to give them, and they left him with sounds of derision. Thus undisturbed and abstracted, he at length turned his attention to the purpose for which he had made this excursion. He put it in his pipe with his bird's-eye, and for some time smoked with great deliberation. He had, as I have said, a problem to solve and a corollary, but the corollary proved—like a lady's postscript—to be the more important of the two. Should he—as his editor had desired—' tone down the severity ' of his dramatic criticism? Certainly not! What! Write to the prompting of something other than his own judgment!—to the dictation of some one other than himself! Surrender his right of opinion, which any young man in the pit could freely exercise! Of what use was criticism if it was not free? He would maintain the birthright of the critic. That meant, therefore, that he must resign his post on the 'Lancashire Gazette,' which implied that he must seek occupation elsewhere. But where? Since ever he had left Oxford and come to Lancashire, he had looked forward to a London career; was the time arrived for that? He doubted it. It would be a perilous thing to launch himself on the wide sea of London journalism with no better recommendation than that he had quarrelled with the editor of the 'Lancashire Gazette.' But if he could not risk the resignation of his present post, he must fall in with the wish of his chief, and 'tone down,' &c.— and that, of course, he could not do. Yet—— And so the discussion with himself went on in the undecisive way we all know.

While he smoked and revolved these things, he let his eyes idly rove about the lake and over the features of a new building which Suffield had reared upon the opposite bank, a building which Ainsworth believed was set apart for some new and secret process of calico-printing. As his eye ranged vaguely from window to window, suddenly he saw, as it were, a vision of a black face and a white turban. What had overcome him that such an hallucination should present itself to him then? He took his pipe from his mouth, rubbed his hand across his eyes, and looked again. The vision had disappeared; but as he continued looking, slow to believe that what he had seen was merely a creature of his brain, he saw it again at another window—again the black head and neck—with the face half averted and the white turban! He looked steadily, and saw the head pass slowly from window to window, as if the person to whom the head was attached were attentively examining everything as he moved along! It was difficult not to believe that he saw a living human being; and yet how was it possible that a black man in a white turban should be alone in a Lancashire mill? It would not be more strange to see some morning a Moorish Kadi sitting cross-legged on the bench of magistrates of the borough.

He jumped up, determined to have his doubt settled, and made his way round towards the building. He was brought up short, however, by finding that the great gates which admitted to the precincts of the works were firmly closed, as was also the little postern against the lodge. It seemed, too, that the lodge and gate keeper must be making holiday with the rest; for no knocking on his door or on the postern brought any response. Ainsworth, therefore, turned away, and went back to the spot under the alders, whence he had seen the vision of the black man. He waited for some time, but no black man reappeared; and then he wandered down the clough.

The more he thought of his vision the more it disturbed him. It disturbed him more than it would have disturbed a man of less knowledge and speculation. He knew, for instance, that Suffield had some secret of his business shut up in that building where he had seen the black man; he knew that in the town there were several Parsee merchants, active with real intellectual activity and crafty with true Eastern craft; and he knew that the Parsees of Bombay were at that hour striving their utmost to compete with Lancashire for the cotton and calico trade of India. What more likely, then, than that a creature of theirs should be commissioned to spy out what he could of Suffield's successful methods? He resolved to seek Suffield out and tell him what he had seen.

He crossed the stream by a narrow footbridge and climbed the opposite side of the clough to enter the park. He crossed into the park by that stile on which Suffield had sat in the early morning, and then, to his amazement, saw sauntering on before him a man in a white turban and a kind of white blouse

girt about with a red sash or *cummerbund.*
He quickened his pace to overtake the man.
When he had overtaken him he was at a loss
what to do.   He could not demand brusquely:
'Are you the person I saw in one of the
buildings of Suffield's works?' That appeared to him uncalled-for rudeness even
to a black man, who is, after all—as the
undergraduate said of his tutor—' a man and
a brother.'   Not knowing what else to do, he
was therefore passing on, when the black man
made him pause.

'Respectable sir,' said he, bowing low,
with his black hands crossed on his white
bosom—' fine Englishman, with regards may
I say?'

Ainsworth stopped, and the black man
smiled upon him in a simple childlike way
that should have banished suspicion. But
Ainsworth felt a stern sense of duty; moreover, although the man's words were in-

telligible, his meaning was not; and he consequently did not smile in return.

'Do you mean,' he asked, 'that you wish to speak to me?'

'Sir,' said Daniel—for of course it was he—'you truly mention it. If you look for the parties of amusement, I beg to say they are almost at the dining off the people, and besides several national foods, curries made by me from fine recipes at your respectable service, sir; hope you like an economical dish which little care and attention is given to it.'

'Thank you very much,' said Ainsworth, feeling that the man meant well, however he expressed himself. 'May I ask if you also belong to the parties of amusement?'

'No, sir,' answered Daniel, smiling again; 'the fact is I myself am servant, cook, *etcetera*, to the Sahib Raynor, now staying at the great Hall.'

'What! Mr. Raynor the traveller? He has come, then?'

'With regard to your speeches, sir, the Sahib Raynor came the day before it was yesterday.'

'And do you,' said Ainsworth, foolishly thinking to catch his black man unawares— 'do you often have business down there at the works all by yourself?'

'Sir,' said Daniel, smiling most serenely, ' I take myself all alone for agreeable walks in the scenery; I range my mind; I improve myself in the great England and Lancashire; and I practise the conversations and the ways and the means. Good-morning; good-bye, sir.'

Bewildered to find the right meaning in that maze of words, and rebuffed in his attempt to catch the man out, Ainsworth said 'Good-bye' somewhat gruffly and went on his way. In the park, outside the lawn before the mansion, he saw there was a great tent pitched, towards which streams of stragglers were setting from all quarters, and in and out of which men and women were hasting and flitting, like bees to and from a hive. It seemed the centre of interest and activity, and towards it, therefore, he bent his steps. While he was yet a good way off, Suffield hailed him from the door of the tent.

'Holloa, Ainsworth! Come along, my son; better late than never.' With him stood a young lady in white—his daughter, Ainsworth could see—and when the young man reached him he continued: 'My little girl here and her cousin called for you at the office to bring you along in the carriage; but you were gone: earlier than usual, eh?'

'I am sorry I missed them,' answered Ainsworth, saluting Suffield's daughter. 'But

I dare say I did leave the office a little earlier than I commonly do.'

But Suffield was evidently thinking of something else already; the thought which would always come uppermost in his mind was how he could do a good turn to a friend, especially to the friend that at the moment was by him.

'You've heard of Lord Clitheroe—the Earl of Padiham's son?' said he, laying his hand on Ainsworth's shoulder and speaking in his ear. 'This is him;' referring with his thumb to a tall, full-bearded young man, who stood a step behind him talking with Miss Suffield, with critical but admiring eyes bent upon her. 'He's a clever fellow; you ought to know him: he's a rising politician.' Then turning, with his hand still on Ainsworth's shoulder, he said—before Ainsworth could utter 'Yea' or 'Nay'—'Clitheroe, let me introduce to you my friend, Mr. Alan Ainsworth. I think you two should know each other.'

It was done easily, without the slightest vulgar touch of ostentation or obsequiousness, as if George Suffield had been to the manner born; which Ainsworth was inclined to wonder at, till he considered that, after all, the best prompters of good manners are a gentle heart and a generous habit.

Lord Clitheroe responded to the introduction as it had been made, easily and frankly. 'Oh, yes,' said he; 'I remember Mr. Ainsworth at Oxford.'

'Oh, ah,' said Suffield; 'sort of college chums.'

'Scarcely so much as that,' said Ainsworth, with a slight hint in his voice of his appreciation of the difference in their rank. 'I think it was only at the Union that Lord Clitheroe and I met.'

'And bitterly denounced each other's politics,' added Lord Clitheroe.

'That's all right,' said Suffield. 'A good stand-up fight of any sort is the best way of beginning to be friends. But Ainsworth's line is different now: he is great as a dramatic critic. Didn't you read the notice of the play in the "Gazette," this morning, Clitheroe?'

'I did,' answered Clitheroe, 'and I liked it very much.'

'That's more than my editor did,' said Ainsworth with a laugh. 'He says I mustn't write like that any more.'

'So ho!' exclaimed Suffield. 'You'll have to cut the "Gazette," then?'

'I have just been turning the matter over,' said Ainsworth, 'considering what I shall do.'

'You must come to London, my lad,' said Suffield, clapping his hand on his shoulder.

' That's the place for you.   I'll manage it for you.'

' You are very good,' said Ainsworth.   ' I dare say it will have to come to that.'

' Of course it will.   But now we are forgetting this spread for the folk.   I think we must all lend a hand, mustn't we, Phemy ?— to get it in order.'

' If you will come with me, Mr. Ainsworth,' said Phemy, ' we shall soon get the other things that are wanted.   We are going to decorate the tables a little, you know, with flowers : our people love flowers.'

' I'm sure you must have taught them that, Miss Suffield,' said Lord Clitheroe gallantly.

' Oh, no, I haven't,' said Phemy, with a candid look of surprise.

So it came to pass that in a minute or two Ainsworth entered with Miss Suffield the ample conservatories attached to the Hall.

They had barely entered when she exclaimed that she had forgotten something.

' Wait here for me,' said she, and fled.

Left alone, he wandered slowly down between the terraces of gorgeous and richly-scented flowers, thinking of nothing in particular, but letting the beauty and the odour of the bewildering array of blooms subdue his senses. Presently he came upon a glass door, which he opened. He found himself in a wide inner apartment of glass and flowers, which he at once recognised as the conservatory immediately annexed to the drawing-room. On the tiled floor were spread costly Persian rugs, and in the centre was a small fountain, in the sunken basin of which grew rare specimens of water-lilies. He was no sooner in than he heard voices, whether in the conservatory or just within the drawing-room he could not tell; for a big flowering magnolia prevented him from seeing any person. He turned to withdraw, but the latch had somehow caught, and the door would not open. He had a mind to go forward, when certain words that caught his ear prevented him.

'Hush! There is some one coming,' said one voice—the voice of Miss Raynor. 'I like you very much,' she continued, evidently in reply to something said by another voice; 'but I prefer you to still be my kind cousin, George. So, please, don't speak to me of these things again.'

'Then, Bell,' said the other voice—the voice of young George Suffield—in an aggrieved and somewhat sulky tone, 'there *is* some one you've got to know in London, and that letter this morning was from him.'

'I think it is unworthy of you, George, to say that,' said Isabel. 'If it were another than you that said it, I should just be silent, and let him believe what he liked. But we are cousins, George; we have grown up together, and I am very sorry I cannot be what you wish; and so I tell you frankly there is no person in London of the kind you mean.'

'If there is not,' urged George, 'why do you refuse to listen to me. See, Bell; I've waited for you ever since I was a little boy; it's not fair—it's not right—of you to say " No " to me so easily and promptly.'

'Oh, George, I don't say it easily nor promptly; I say it reluctantly and I say it with pain. If I were a young, thoughtless girl, and did not believe that a woman should feel towards a man she means to live with always very much more than I feel towards you, I might even have said " Yes." '

'You may say " Yes " yet, Bell. We shall understand each other better after this. Do not answer me at all now. Wait a while;

wait a year, if you like. Do that—won't you, Bell?'

'Very well,' said Isabel, after a moment's hesitation. 'If it will make you happy, George, I'll wait.'

'Thank you, Bell. Thank you—and bless you.'

'Don't, George,' said she, as if in repulse of some slight attempt to embrace her. 'Be good, and control yourself.'

Then George withdrew by the drawing-room, and Isabel appeared round the magnolia and stood before Ainsworth, whose thought and pulse were in a turmoil.

'Forgive me,' he stammered with his eyes down: he did not dare to raise them. 'I wandered in here by this door; and when I heard voices and tried to go back the door would not open; and I could not go on and appear before you.'

She said not a word, nor stirred; and he

raised his eyes to look at her. Upon that
—as if the expression of his face and the
light in his eyes at once betrayed him to her
—she was suffused with an overwhelming
blush; she looked at the closed door behind
him, and turned and fled like a stricken
deer.

Yes; Ainsworth now understood, without
recognising, himself. The jealousy, sharp
and wild, which seized him when he discovered that another man was seeking to win
this lady, and the mad suspicion that others
also might think her love worth winning,
precipitated feelings which had long been
hanging about him like a haze. Now he
saw in a burning light that it was a matter
of the supremest moment that Isabel Raynor
should love him, and him alone. Now he
felt himself a new, a stronger, a more resolute, a more clear-seeing and alert man. His
problem was solved and its corollary. His way

was made plain before him : he must leave Lancashire and the 'Lancashire Gazette,' and compel reluctant Fortune to befriend him in that London where Isabel lived and moved and had her being.

CHAPTER VIII

AT THE GREAT WHITE FEAST

IN a few seconds Euphemia came and released Ainsworth from his embarrassing confinement. She laughed at his serious and wondering face, thinking it was due to anxiety lest she should not find him.

'But,' said she, peeping round the magnolia, 'you might have got out through the drawing-room: I see the door is open.'

'Oh, yes,' said he; 'I daresay I might have got out through the drawing-room.'

He helped her to collect and to carry out such flowering plants as she selected, but all in so absent-minded a way that still she laughed and chaffed him; and he smiled and bore it, for he was so possessed and inter-penetrated with the glow of his new feeling that he was insensible to the shafts of ridicule. He was in love, and love was in him, and he knew it. For let it be noted that there is an important difference in what are called ' affairs of the heart' between most men and women. Man as man is open, direct, and simple in his feelings; woman as woman is secret, involved, and complex. So it comes to pass that when a man is really touched with love's fitful fever he is commonly able to diagnose himself; he knows what is the matter with him, and acts accordingly. A woman, on the other hand, seldom recognises when she is in love; she may be very far gone, plunged beyond hope of recovery, and yet not know it; and even when she may suspect where she is, she clouds, obfuscates, or glozes the fact to herself, and calls it something else—until the man speaks, and then !——

Thus the twinge caused by the talk overheard in the conservatory had made Ainsworth recognise what had happened to him; and, recognising it, he was resolved to win the only assuagement possible—the love of the woman who had touched his heart. Isabel, on her part, was troubled and distressed at what had occurred; she saw no reason, nor had she any inclination, to blame Ainsworth for it; but she began from that hour to take more note of him, to underline, so to say, her interest in him, without in the least suspecting what had happened, or was happening, to herself.

In something less than half an hour Ainsworth's journeyings with Euphemia and the flower-pots to and from the marquee were at an end, the tables were set forth, and the guests were all assembled, and were settling down into their places; then he chanced to glance across a space of table and he suddenly came to himself. He knew that a man whom he felt must have been he had been for some time hurrying to and fro, but whether in the body or out of the body he could not tell, and what he had been doing he could not tell; now, however, he saw plainly where he was and knew clearly who he was; for there, a little way off on the other side of the table, stood she—the one *she* in the world for him! —her face flushed and smiling above her white diaphanous raiment, and her eyes sparkling like glorious jewels beneath her crown of dark hair. She was in reality just as she had been half an hour before, save, perhaps, for the new animation of her bearing; but to Ainsworth's inspired eyes she appeared transfigured into a vision of the supremest loveliness of life and health, of body and mind. The sight of her intoxicated and dazzled him, till she glanced his way and their eyes met, when the frank intelligence and confidence of her look soothed and steadied him.

There was neither time nor opportunity then for other communication; for part of the fun and formula of that feast was that the chief members of the household and the chief guests must act as stewards. At the head of one table Suffield generously carved a great joint of beef; at the head of the second his son carved another joint; and at a third the mistress of the house herself dispensed smaller dishes; while her daughter and her niece, Lord Clitheroe and Mr. Ainsworth, the clergyman of the church and the minister of the chapel and their 'respectable' wives—as Daniel would have said—aided the domestics of the house, hung round the tables, and saw that the feasters had what they desired to eat and drink. In passing thus to and fro, Ainsworth hovered near Isabel's sacred presence; yet not too near, nor even as near as he might have gone, for he felt there was a line, to pass beyond which would have been familiar, if not rude. The feasters were all heads of households in the village—fathers and mothers, and some grandfathers and grandmothers; for the un-married and the young were still kicking their heels outside, waiting for their turn at the tables, even as they were waiting for their complete innings at life. While the elder people still kept their seats and the younger still hung outside, a foreman got upon his feet to propose the health of 'oor mester and mistress;' and Suffield responded in a speech which took and held Ainsworth's attention. He had never before had the opportunity of considering his friend as a public speaker, and now as he listened he was surprised and delighted to think he had in him the essentials of a popular orator. He spoke clearly, in simple, straightforward language, with unconscious dignity and sweetness of temper, and with feeling and humour ; so that his audience followed him with cheerful understanding, and now felt the springing of moisture to the eyes and now broke into the heartiest laughter. His anecdotes were naturally the best appreciated parts of his speech ; to that audience they were as the plums of a pudding ; for they were told in the strong and racy Lancashire dialect— which it would be impossible to reproduce here intelligibly—and they were seized on by the untravelled and unlearned natives as their exclusive property. While they roared with laughter, they glanced round upon their attendant superiors with the clear meaning in their eyes : 'What do you think of that for a story ? Of course you don't understand it, but we do.'

Ainsworth paid heed to all these things, and in so doing he moved—perhaps not quite unwittingly—closer to Isabel. When the speech was finished and the cheering had ceased, he was fluttered and delighted anew by her turning to him with a gracious smile and a divine blush, and saying on the impulse : 'What a delightful speech! Don't you think so? I had no idea that Uncle George was so good a speaker.'

'Nor I,' answered Ainsworth with pleased alacrity, and his words came in a nervous, hurried stream. 'It is a model speech for the occasion—simple, pathetic, and humorous. And such capital stories he told! I didn't understand them a bit myself—I haven't Lancashire enough, though I am half a Lancashire man—but I saw they were caught and understood by all the folk. An admirable speech. Mr. Suffield ought to become a great platform orator.'

'Do you think so, really?' asked Isabel with a touch of deference, as if to better-instructed opinion than her own. 'I should like to hear him make a speech in Parliament.'

'Ah,' said Ainsworth, 'I believe that's not quite the same thing. I don't know of myself, but I've always heard, that a man may be an admirable platform speaker, and quite fail as a speaker in the House. I can quite understand that; can't you?'

'Oh yes. Just as a clergyman may be a very good preacher, but a duffer—duffer is the word, is it not?'—he laughed more hilariously than was quite necessary—'a duffer when he gets up to speak among his brethren.'

'That's it. You put it excellently. Of course, I don't mean that Mr. Suffield would be a failure; but, as you so well said, success of the one kind doesn't necessarily imply success of the other.'

With a woman's fine intuition, Isabel

perceived his nervous eagerness to please, and in a measure understood its cause. She therefore became more self-possessed, indulgent, and expansive, though she did not dare to let the talk drop, for fear of the reflection that might spring up in the pause.

'I can't,' said she, 'know so much of these things as you——'

'But why not?' he interrupted. 'You seem to me to be thoroughly acquainted with everything, and to be able to set men right in many things—you do.'

'Really, Mr. Ainsworth,' she laughed—a laugh which showed that the praise, though extravagant, was agreeable—'if I could believe you mean what you say, I should be puffed up with conceit.'

'But I *do* mean what I say—I mean everything that I say,' he urged fervently.

'And so you are waiting to see me puffed up?'—she laughed again.

'No, no, no; you are too wise, you have too much ballast to be puffed up.'

'You mean,' said she, 'that I am too wise to be puffed up, and even if I were puffed up I have too much ballast to be carried away? Really, really, Mr. Ainsworth, your compliment after all proves gross and equivocal!'

'You are right, you are right, of course. But at the same time you prove the truth of what I said—that you can set men right in many things—don't you see? But you were going to say something when I interrupted you.'

'Oh, I was going to say only that, though I know nothing of politics, I think it is possible that Uncle George may be a success in Parliament. He will try hard to be, I know, for my aunt has that ambition for him, and he always likes to please her.'

'That's very beautiful of him, now!'

exclaimed he—'after so many years of married life.'

'Yes,' said she, as if she had been suddenly provoked to consider the point, 'I suppose it is.'

'Not many couples, I fancy,' said he, 'have such confidence and belief in each other after a quarter of a century of marriage.'

'No; I daresay not,' said she, and showed an inclination to plunge into a reverie on the matter. But she shook off the inclination, and said: 'That's chiefly why uncle has taken a great house in London.'

'Oh!' exclaimed he. '*Has* he taken a house in London?'

'Didn't you know?' said she. 'The town-house of Lord Clitheroe's father, the Earl of Padiham. And the family is going to live there regularly—except George; he is going to remain here and manage all the business, I believe.'

While the conversation had been in progress, faint blushes had been coming and going on Isabel's countenance, but on the chance mention of George's name, a blinding blush swept over her, making her look down in confusion and Ainsworth look away in sympathy. He relieved her, however, by continuing the talk without heeding what she had said of George.

' I'm going to London, too,' said he.

' Are you really?' she asked, with a quick look of lively interest. ' I had not heard of it before.'

' I only resolved on it to-day,' said he; and added hurriedly, on the sudden fear that she would connect his resolution with the scene in the conservatory, ' I've had a word or two with my editor, and I've practically no alternative but resign my post: I must either change my style of criticism or go. I prefer to go.'

'Of course,' said Isabel, at length showing that unconsciousness of herself which was one of her chief charms.

'I hope,' said he, 'when we are both in London I shall often have the pleasure of meeting you.'

'No doubt we shall meet,' said she, looking thoughtful. 'But—excuse my saying it— I hope you have something in prospect in London.'

'Well,' said he with a laugh, 'I believe there are ever so many birds in the bush, though I confess I have not one in the hand.'

'You have the Lancashire bird still in your hand—have you not?' she said.

'You mean to suggest,' said he, 'that I am not wise in letting it go? There are risks, of course; but every movement is attended with some risk, and,' he continued with intention, 'I have reached a point in my life when I prefer to run a risk. But after all,

from my position on the " Lancashire Gazette,"
I am not quite prospectless ; and Mr. Suffield
has given me encouragement.'

' Uncle George,' said Isabel, ' is always so
good.'

' He is absolutely the best man I know,'
said Ainsworth.

And thus the conversation came to an end
with the recurrence of their duties as stewards;
so that it seemed all the more to Ainsworth
like an interlude of heavenly music in the
commonplace jangle and dull jar of average
daily duty. The second relay of feasters had
taken the places of the first while our pair
were talking, and now they were completely
settled and eager for the good things of the
Suffield dispensation to be set before them.
The second turn at the tables passed like the
first, and then the feasters rose and went forth
to play. When they were gone, Ainsworth,
finding himself at length hungry, proffered a

request to Miss Raynor, near whom he still maintained himself.

'Do you think,' said he, 'that I might have something to eat? I've had no lunch.'

'Certainly,' said she at once. 'I suppose aunt must have thought you had lunch in town. We had luncheon early and quick to be ready for this.'

She ran off to her aunt and presently returned, saying that she was deputed to attend to his wants.

That would be scarcely worth chronicling were it not that 'the green-eyed monster' was looking forth from young George Suffield's countenance, with consequences that shall duly appear. All the while Ainsworth and Isabel had conversed George had observed them, and thought with a pang that they seemed very friendly and pleased with each other; and now that they went together to a side-table, while all were fast withdrawing from the marquee, and sat down—Ainsworth to eat and drink, and both to talk—the green-eyed monster's wasting heart beat in George's bosom in place of the young man's own honest organ. He could hear before he also withdrew that they were only talking of things literary and dramatic, but still they appeared to him more friendly and better pleased with each other than was necessary.

Something less than half an hour later Ainsworth was passing alone from the marquee to where the Whitsuntide revellers were romping and playing, when he was suddenly reminded of the purpose with which he had entered Holdsworth Park. Amid the new emotions and events of the past hour or two he had forgotten the existence of the black man, till now he saw him again pass blandly across his vision. He also was moving towards the crowd of holiday-makers; but he halted a little way off and stood with his black hands behind him, smiling and nodding indulgently, like a comment and a query of the ancient and mysterious East concerning the youthful, rude, and noisy West. Ainsworth passed him quickly by; and thinking of what Isabel had told him of George's approaching investiture with supreme authority at the mills, to George Suffield he immediately went. He was somewhat puzzled with his reception. George was commonly very cordial with him; he was now cold: he was commonly frank and talkative; he was now silent and suspicious. But Ainsworth set his changed behaviour down to the account of the scene in the conservatory, and forgave him.

'Do you know,' he asked, 'that black man standing over there?'

'Yes, of course,' answered George; 'he's my uncle's servant.'

'Oh, then,' said Ainsworth, 'perhaps you know of his having been in one of your mills

—the special one against the dam—an hour or two ago?'

'Been where?' asked George, at length giving his real attention.

Then Ainsworth related what he had seen; and George, without remark and without hesitation, called Daniel, who came at once to the summons.

'Where were you two hours ago, Trichy?' asked George.

'Sahib George,' began Daniel, with a careless sidelong regard upon Ainsworth from his fine orbs, 'it is troublesome to remember all and many things; but the same time I must say that I have been taking myself for much interval for agreeable walks in the respected places of interest—in the valley with the waters and the animals with long back legs, etcetera.'

'Have you been in the mill by the lake? —on the brink of the dam?'

'Where is the mill? Where is the lake? Where is the—*what*?' asked Daniel with a smile—a smile of ingenuous Eastern subtlety. 'I am regret to say that an Englishman says "damn" to turn away his feeling, but I am not sufficient to understand the meaning of the other. What is "dam" now?'

'Have you been in any of the mill-buildings in the valley?' asked George weakly.

'With regard may I say—is it able to enter myself in any of your English buildings when they are closed without the key? Have I the favour of the key? So just may I ask where can I be?'

'Answer me "Yes" or "No"!' persisted George; 'have you been in any of the buildings? Yes or No?'

'No, Sahib George,' answered Daniel directly enough, and with the fullest, steadiest eye imaginable.

'There; you hear,' said George to Ainsworth; and adding with a bitter kind of enjoyment that surprised himself, I have no doubt: 'Don't you think you might have been mistaken? People are so often mistaken in what they fancy they have heard and understood; and if the ears should deceive you so much, why should not the eyes?'

'I don't think,' said Ainsworth, the more obstinately because of the singular tone of young Suffield's observation, 'that I can have been mistaken. I saw him as plainly as I see you.'

By that the eager conclave had naturally attracted attention, and seemed likely to attract an audience also.

'Anything the matter?' asked the elder Suffield, approaching with Uncle Harry, the Sahib Raynor.

'Only that Mr. Ainsworth,' said George

lightly, ' thinks he saw Trichy in the new mill.'

' But how could Trichy get in there?' asked Suffield.

' Ah, how?' asked George, in a semi-scoffing tone, which nettled Ainsworth.

' Of course,' said he, 'it does not matter to me; but I thought it of consequence to you, Mr. Suffield; and I am completely certain I saw this—er—black—I mean, dark—gentleman in the new mill.'

' This is serious,' said Suffield; ' this must be inquired into. What do you think, Harry?'

But before Uncle Harry could reply, George had again spoken, out of an absurd desire to oppose by any means, or to mitigate or make of no account, anything that Ainsworth might say.

' If the thing has been done, father,' said he, ' no inquiry can undo it. If the steed has been stolen, no inquiry into the question of whether the thief entered or no can bring the steed back. If Daniel·Trichinopoly has been in that mill, then I suggest that the only remedy is to swear Daniel Trichinopoly into our service—to do his duty faithfully, and to reveal no secrets of our business or of our manufacture.'

' Ah,' said Suffield, ' that sounds not a bad idea. What do you think, Harry?'

'Oh,' said Uncle Harry, 'Daniel will swear.' Then he asked Daniel, in the man's native Tamil, if he would like to enter the Suffield service; to which Daniel replied in the same tongue that he would, and that he would be faithful·as the ass that treadeth out the corn. ('The seed,' said he, 'of the banyan is small, but the tree gives a great shade.') 'He says he is willing and glad to enter your service, George. Take him by all means—with my blessing. Take him, and swear him in by any oath you like; they're all alike to him. And,' continued the traveller to Daniel, ' come to me to-night, and we'll settle our accounts.'

' The Sahib,' said Daniel in his Tamil, bowing with his hands crossed upon his breast, ' is wise and comprehends. Having set out to run, is it well to be behind one who wishes to rest by the way? Moreover, as the Sahib knows, life without action is like a curry without *seerakam*.'

' It is well,' said Mr. Raynor, also in Tamil. ' See that you maintain the hand of the diligent and the heart of the honest, or you will be as the hare that of its own accord ran into the cook-room.'

Having so said, he turned aside to receive a telegram brought by a servant ; and thus, on the prompting of a moment of pique and whim, without any reflection, was the dusky and mysterious Daniel enlisted in the service of the great house of Suffield.

Uncle Harry handed the telegram to his brother-in-law: it was an intimation from the Royal Geographical Society that Mr. Raynor's promised lecture on his travels had been set down for an early date, and that his presence was desired to make the necessary arrangements as soon as possible.

'I shall go and pack at once,' said Uncle Harry, 'and catch the evening mail.—Come, Daniel.'

'You can surely wait till to-morrow, Harry,' said Suffield. 'I wanted you to make properly the acquaintance of my friend Ainsworth here—have a good talk with him, you know, and so on. And I was looking forward to a nice party at dinner.'

'I hope,' said Mr. Raynor, turning frankly to Ainsworth, 'to have abundant opportunity to enjoy Mr. Ainsworth's company in London. And you know, George, I always like to carry out an intention while it's hot.'

' Ah, well,' said Suffield, ' if you must, you must. I know you're as ill to hold as a tewing horse.'

' And in any case, Mr. Suffield,' said Ainsworth, ' I couldn't stay to dinner, as you have been kindly suggesting. I must get back to the office to my work.'

' Well now,' said Suffield, ' this is what I call a miserably docked tail of a Whitsuntide festival.'

Ainsworth was a little sore about young George's behaviour towards him, and presently he said his adieus and departed to the station—not without hope of meeting Miss Raynor as he crossed the park. But though he lingered and walked as wide as he dared, he saw nothing of her, and he returned to town in a somewhat despondent and lonely mood, but still resolved to sever his connection with the ' Lancashire Gazette ' at once.

CHAPTER IX

WHAT CAME OF A LECTURE AT THE ROYAL GEOGRAPHICAL

A WEEK later, all the Suffield family, except George, were established in Rutland Gate. They had hurried up to London to attend Uncle Harry's meeting with the Royal Geographical Society. That took place in the rooms of the Society on the evening of the day they arrived, and all three were present—agog to listen to their relative's account of his latest travels—and Miss Raynor was also among them : she had been in London attending to her school duties for two or three days already.

' George would have enjoyed this,' said

Suffield, looking round upon the more or less distinguished company of ladies and gentlemen. 'It's a pity he couldn't be spared from the works for a day; but he couldn't, you know, at the present time. I say he couldn't be spared,' he repeated, half-aside to Isabel.

'No, uncle,' said Isabel, feeling compelled to say something to that direct appeal, 'I suppose he couldn't.'

'If Mr. Ainsworth is in London,' said Mrs. Suffield, giving a glance at her niece, 'he might have come to-night.'

'Has he come to London yet?' asked Isabel, without attempting to conceal her interest.

'No,' answered Suffield, 'not yet. He wrote to me a day or two ago that he would not be up for a week or so. But here's your uncle going to begin.'

Since this is not a geographical treatise, nor a record of the proceedings in Old

Burlington Street, but only a story concerning a few people in whom we are deeply interested, mention is made here of Mr. Raynor's address to the Royal Geographical Society only because of one particular, and, it may seem, obscure, result of its delivery. It marked an auspicious change in the relations between Isabel and her uncle, and by that token it was the determining point of her history. I must not, however, be supposed to mean that Isabel was in any wise more conscious that she had taken a new departure than is the moorland rill when its course is deflected by a stone, and it thenceforth flows in another direction than that in which it had set out; I merely use the historian's privilege of laying the finger on some small fact which might be impatiently skipped as of no consequence, and saying: 'Note this: it is a point (or an angle) of event or opportunity.'

Isabel listened to her uncle's adventures in the Shan States with unwavering attention. Everything he said was of supreme interest to her, first because she was of the rare kind of young lady that, with a romantic imagination, has an omnivorous appetite for facts; and second, because her uncle had been, like Aeneas, 'a great part' of all he related. Moreover, she had a tolerably clear idea of the whereabouts of the Shan States, and of their characteristic features, which, it may be cheerfully granted, most of the guests of the Royal Geographers had not. Was it not natural, therefore, that Mr. Raynor, casting his shrewd eye round as his discourse progressed, and remarking the politely-veiled looseness of attention and dulness of understanding of rows of well-dressed people, and even the wandering gaze and the ill-suppressed yawn of those of his own household, should fix his eye with satisfaction and pleasure on the intelligent and unweariedly attentive face of his brother's daughter? The wall of dislike and suspicion which he had built between his niece and himself had already begun to crumble under various influences. The grievance against his brother, which he had nursed and kept warm in his foreign solitude, had been discouraged and refused attention by his kindly brother-in-law, and he had asked himself—on Suffield's suggestion—'Was it, after all, fair that the girl should be held in cold disgrace because of the wrong done by her parents?' Moreover, he was fain to confess to himself, after his few days' close observation of Isabel in Lancashire, that he had been mistaken in thinking her pragmatical, conceited, and ambitious; and since he had come to London he had recalled in the loneliness of his hotel the unconscious, pathetic, gentle inquiry he had now and again seen in her eye—'What have done that my father's brother should treat me so coldly?'—and he had felt ashamed of himself. Now, on this Royal Geographical evening, Isabel finally conquered, and won her uncle's regard much as Desdemona won Othello's love, by her simple, engrossed attention to his tale of adventure, peril, and discovery. And just in such degree as Uncle Harry had been crabbed, reserved, and suspicious hitherto, he became open, generous, and trusting.

All five rode to Rutland Gate together from Old Burlington Street in the roomy Suffield carriage, and Uncle Harry chaffed his sister and his brother-in-law in remote terms for their inattention to his discourse. He suggested that, being now established in an Earl's house, they felt justified in being supercilious; that they had eaten a dinner of aristocratic length and *bourgeois* substance; that the air of the lecture-room had been soporific, and the dresses of the ladies distracting ; and so forth.

'Well, you see, Harry,' said Suffield, 'you struck a note above my understanding rather. I don't know much about geography ; and for all I know, your Shan States may be next door to Timbuctoo.'

'Ah, but, George,' said Harry, 'you'd have wanted to know where they were and all about them, if you had heard that they grew cotton or wanted calico.'

'I should that, lad,' answered Suffield ; 'I should, I confess.'

'You see, Harry,' said Mrs. Suffield, 'George and I are both getting too old to care for knowledge for its own sake.'

'That's just it,' said Suffield. 'But here's a young lady'—leaning forward and laying his hand on Isabel's—'that's a regular cormorant for knowledge. Now *she* listened to you. Didn't you see it? You should be satisfied, I think, if nobody else had heard a word you said.'

'I saw it,' answered Uncle Harry promptly and warmly, but with a touch of shyness, 'and I was more than satisfied—I was flattered.'

'Oh, Uncle Harry!' exclaimed Isabel; she was too surprised and delighted to say more then.

'I believe,' said Aunt Joanna, 'if Uncle Harry were the Royal Geographical Society, he would give you a gold medal, Isabel, for your attention.'

'I would, certainly,' asseverated Uncle Harry.

'I have had some school prizes in my time,' laughed Isabel, 'and I suppose I worked for them; but a gold medal would be the most remarkable and the least deserved of them all. I listened to uncle's lecture because I was interested.'

'You are fond of travel, are you?' asked her uncle.

'I don't know,' she answered, 'because I never have travelled. But I am fond of books of travel——'

'What books are you *not* fond of, Beli?' asked Euphemia from her corner.

'—— and I have to teach geography, you know,' continued Isabel.

'Ah, of course she has!' said Suffield; 'so it's not so much a case of knowledge for its own sake, after all.'

'But I don't suppose, Uncle George,' said she, 'I shall ever be able to use all I've learned about the Shan States from Uncle Harry—though there was one thing I didn't quite understand.'

'And what was that, my dear?' asked Uncle Harry, all agog to explain.

Talking thus, they reached Rutland Gate and sat down to a morsel of supper; and still

Isabel and her uncle—her new-found uncle, it seemed to her—talked ; and then they all went to bed very tired, but very happy— none better pleased at the turn things had taken than the excellent Suffield.

Next morning, Isabel had to be off betimes to attend to her duties at the Ladies' College. When she returned weary to her lodgings in the Marylebone Road late in the afternoon, she had an agreeable surprise. On the mantelpiece of her little sitting-room there awaited her a letter. She did not recog- nise the handwriting on the envelope, but on opening it she found a bank-note for twenty pounds and a note from her Uncle Harry.

'My dear niece,' he wrote, 'I am sending you your gold medal in a handy transmutable form. You can buy a frock or something with it. I should like to come and drink a cup of tea and have a long talk with you, if I

may, to-morrow afternoon.—Your loving
uncle,

'HARRY RAYNOR.'

Isabel sat down for an instant to endure
the happiness that filled her. She was of
those bright, well-constituted souls that delight to believe that all people—especially their
kindred and those they must associate with—
are more or less good. It had pained her to
have to think hardly and grudgingly of her
uncle, and now that she could think well of
him, she rejoiced all the more because she
had formerly thought ill. She did not lay
the change in his behaviour to the account of
any merit of her own; she did not even stay
to remark that he had changed; she only
took blame to herself that she had until now
mistaken him.

'How good, how kind of him!' she said
to herself, glancing again at his note; and
she was not thinking of the money he had

sent—part of which she had already mentally set aside for her father—but of the disposition that had prompted the gift and the accompanying affectionate expressions.

She at once drew up to the table and wrote a little letter of thanks and of invitation: she would expect, she said, to see her uncle at five o'clock the following afternoon.

And at five o'clock the following afternoon he came. He pressed her hand affectionately, and then he fidgeted about her little sitting-room for some time, peeping into the books on her side-table, reading the backs of the volumes in her bookcase, and looking at the prints on the walls.

'Pretty comfortable, eh?' he asked.

'It suits me very well, uncle,' she answered. 'As well, that is,' she continued with a laugh, 'as my landlady will permit. The tear of reproach is constantly trembling in her eye ; she thinks it so improper, poor dear soul, in a young lady—not a young woman ; she makes the distinction—to live alone. I have literally had to wring a latch-key out of her. And whenever I come home late, I find her sitting up for me ; and she says " Good-night " with such a sigh of relief, that I am tempted to pass upstairs whistling and bang my door like a man. Poor woman ! I am on her conscience, I know ; and she tries to get me to believe that I am always trembling on the verge of disgrace or ruin. But it's handy here for the college, and it's cheap.'

'Hum ; yes,' murmured her uncle. Then suddenly turning to her and taking her hand he said : ' My dear, I have an apology to make. Down at your Uncle Suffield's place you no doubt thought me very cold and distant to you.' Isabel blushed and said nothing, though she looked him frankly in the face : she could not deny that she had thought something of the kind. 'Of course you did,' he went on ; 'and I was, I know. I haven't much excuse, but such as it is, I give it. You reminded me very much of a woman—a girl—that once—years ago— treated me badly—at least, worse than I deserved. That's all. The impression has worn off ; I see you are not like her in the least. So let us be friends, and say no more about it ;' and again he warmly pressed her hand.

Isabel returned his pressure, saying : 'I am not sorry you have told me that, uncle ; though I *am* sorry you have told it me as an apology. Everyone has a right to form an opinion of another.'

'Even a wrong one ?' queried her uncle.

'Even a wrong one, surely, uncle,' said she, 'if it be formed on what appear sufficient grounds.'

' Ah, that's just it ! ' said her uncle.

She made no other allusion to that past of his of which his words had given her a hint; but henceforward it invested him in her eyes with a new sentimental interest, in which the strongest-minded woman likes to indulge.

And then they sat down to tea and became very friendly. They talked freely and almost without pause of many things, Isabel perceiving that she pleased her uncle both with her opinions and her expression of them, and resuming, therefore, more and more of her bright, fresh self. As they thus talked, he suddenly posed her with a question: ' What would you do if you had a great deal of money ? '

' What would you call " a great deal " ? ' she asked, thinking of her salary, the twenty pounds she had just received, and her father.

' Well, not so much as your Uncle George

has tied up in his mills,' answered he, ' but enough, say, to bring a yearly income of about three thousand pounds.—Would *you* call that " a great deal," or not ? '

' I would,' said Isabel, with her eye not really on herself, but on her uncle. ' And if I had so much, the first thing I should do, I believe, would be to make myself very comfortable, especially if my life hitherto had been, rather hard, and busy, and bare. If I had a taste for books, I should buy books— beautiful books, and rare books ; and if I had a taste for pictures, I should surround myself with fine pictures—not very expensive pic- tures, necessarily, by famous artists, but pic- tures that pleased me whether they were by popular painters or no; and so on with furni- ture, and china, and carpets, and beautiful things of all kinds.   And then if I liked good dinners, I should have them.'

' Dinners, too ! ' laughed her uncle. ' My

dear, you will permit me to say that your tastes appear masculine.'

'Well,' she answered, 'is it not of a man I am thinking?'

'I see!' he cried. 'You are thinking of me! But I wish you to think of yourself. I want to know what you would do with so much money.'

'Truly, uncle,' she answered after a moment's consideration, 'if you want a serious answer—I don't know. I should feel it a great, an anxious, responsibility. And, since I haven't so much money, nor am ever likely to have'—had she then been looking at her uncle she might have caught a suspicious twinkle from his eye—'why should I bother to inquire of myself what I should do with it?'

'But,' he urged, 'wouldn't you see that all your own people wanted for nothing that they needed or would like?'

'Of course,' she answered; 'but that goes as much without saying as that I should have my own breakfast and dinner, and buy clothes for myself. One's own people ought, I think, to come before all others.'

'Quite so,' said her uncle.—'Well, now, your aunt told me to bring you along to dinner to-night—if you could spare the time—so, if you don't object, we'll walk to Rutland Gate and talk this matter out by the way.—You like walking, I hope?' he asked, seeing something like hesitation on her face.

'Oh yes, uncle,' she answered; 'I like walking, and I'll go with you. But will you let me write a note first? It will only take me two or three minutes.'

This was the business she had turned her thought on: she had promised when in Lancashire to communicate again with her father—or with the person who represented himself as such—as soon as she returned to London; she had been back several days, but she had been able to do nothing for want of money ; now, however, that she had money in abundance, she would let no more days slip by without communicating. She therefore sat down at her side-table and wrote a hasty note to the following effect : 'If you will call at your tobacconist's to-morrow evening, about the time of the last post, you will receive something from me.' She was determined to be resolved whether this man who wrote to her was her father or no, and her plan was, not to send money in the letter she promised, but to be in the tobacconist's shop with sufficient money in her hand at the time she named, and to speak to the person who inquired for her letter ; if that person could satisfy her he was her father, she knew what she would do ; if he could not, she still knew what she would do.

Her note she took out in her hand and posted as she passed along with her uncle. But that very night she had a singular and significant adventure which somewhat modified her expectation of her father

CHAPTER X

'THE ONLY WOMAN IN THE WORLD'

WHEN about ten o'clock that night the great front-door of the house in Rutland Gate was swung open by the attendant footman to permit Miss Raynor to pass out, it was discovered that the weather was wet. It had been a cold day for June, with the wind from the north-east ; and now the wind had shifted into the south-east, bringing a little warmer air laden with fine rain. Seeing that, Mr. Raynor, who had accompanied his niece to the door— her other uncle was already become sedulous in the House of Commons—wished to send her to her lodgings in a cab, which the attendant footman professed a desire to call; but Miss Raynor insisted on going home afoot.

'I prefer to walk,' said she, ' and by myself, thank you, uncle. I shall not get wet; I am shamefully well protected from the rain, with both umbrella and mackintosh.'

So she had her way, and the door closed behind her. She had something of her uncle Suffield's habit of quoting to herself scraps from her reading—scraps which sounded more or less applicable to the occasion. As she departed from the house, holding her skirts as free of her heels as possible, she quoted with a low laugh to herself: 'Go call a coach, and let a coach be called; and let the man that calleth be the caller.'

'Cab, miss?' said the driver of a loitering hansom, as she crossed to enter the Park by the Prince of Wales's Gate.

'No, thank you,' she cheerfully replied; and the cabman drew up his horse to see her

disappear into the comparative darkness of the
Park, and said to a comrade who had loitered
up with another cab : ' P'raps she can afford
a keb, and p'raps she can't.   P'raps she's a
lady, and p'raps she ain't nobody in particular.
Anyhow, she's a fine young woman, and she
'adn't ought to be a-walkin' in the Park all
alone by herself.   'Swelp me !   If I 'adn't my
keb I'd offer to escorch her myself.'

Isabel had quick ears. She overheard, but
she was only amused ; and she held on her
way to the right.   Her nearest route—and
despite the dark and wet she saw no reason
for diverging from it—was round the eastern
end of the Serpentine, and thence directly to
the Marble Arch.   She had passed the
Serpentine—thinking how like an enchanted
lake it looked in that half-light that hung over
London, and with the soft and velvety black-
ness of the trees that begirt it—and was
stepping briskly along the narrow path that

led to the great Archway, when a poor, meagre creature, shuffling by, suddenly snatched her umbrella from her easy hand and fled over the grass.

'The scoundrel!' exclaimed a man who almost as suddenly appeared before her and dashed after the thief. In a few seconds he was up with him, had caught him, and was leading him back to Isabel, himself carrying the recovered umbrella. The victorious stranger had led his captive but a few paces when he wrenched himself free and again fled over the grass. The stranger hesitated an instant whether he should again pursue him, but Isabel called : 'Please let him go!' and he returned, carefully carrying the closed umbrella as if it were of the most precious and fragile nature.

'Madam, permit me,' he said in a rich, genteel voice, which, though somewhat shaken and husky, had the exactitude and modulation of an elocutionist's. He put up the umbrella and handed it to her with a bow of great propriety.

In the dim light she could only see that the polite stranger had a very red and rather puffy face, that his ungloved hand trembled a good deal, and that his spare figure was closely buttoned in a frock-coat against the weather.

'Thank you very much,' said she, 'for your bravery and your kindness.'

'Madam,' said he with solemn deliberation, 'I can never bear to see a lady in distress.'

'Oh, but I was not at all in distress, thank you,' said she. 'If anyone is in distress it must be that poor man, and he has lost his plunder after all.'

'He may have been a deserving man,' said he ; 'but I need not remind you that appearances are frequently deceitful, madam.

Meanwhile, may I accompany you to the broader, better-lighted, and more frequented thoroughfare; it is not wise—if you will permit me to say so—in a lady to perambulate these unfrequented paths alone.’

The man was polite, and seemed harmless, and she thought it would be sheer rudeness to refuse his request, especially since the broader thoroughfare was but a few yards off; so she assented by turning off in that direction. Walking by her side he seemed to halt a little and to lean hard upon his cane.

‘I hope,’ said she, ‘you have not hurt yourself in running after that man?’

‘No, madam,’ he answered. ‘It is only a touch of rheumatism that occasionally supervenes in such weather as the present. I have travelled the round earth over and have passed through numerous hardships, but I never knew what rheumatism was until a year or two agone, when I was camping out in the wilds of America.'

'The round earth over'—where had she heard that phrase? It sounded as if it had once been spoken in her ear. And the man's voice with its cadences and its superfluous fluency—did not that also sound familiar? But the frequented thoroughfare was now reached, and she stopped and signified that there they must part.

'I am exceedingly obliged to you,' said she, tempted a little to imitate his grandiloquence, 'for your polite attentions;' and she bowed, and was passing on.

'Madam,' said he, 'grant me a moment.'

'Yes?' said she.

'You are well-protected against the weather, madam,' said he with a bow, doffing his hat—and then she saw he was partially bald, and that he had a moustache as fiercely and inconsequently bristling, and over it a nose as fiery as Bardolph's own, while his dark eyes shone with a wandering but not unkindly light.

'Yes ; I am,' said she.

'You perceive I am not ;' and he showed the thin and frayed skirt of his frock-coat.

'I am sorry,' said she, 'that you are likely to spoil my opinion of you.'

'You cannot, madam,' said he, 'be sorrier than I. But I can conceive you are generous and sympathetic, and by no means prudish.'

'Well, what then ? What do you wish of me ? '

'Between ourselves, madam, I should like to achieve some refreshment. A bottle of Burgundy is excellent, but, failing that, a glass of Scotch whisky—with water—is not to be despised.'

Isabel found her pocket and her purse, and gave him a shilling.

'Madam,' said he, accepting it, and again doffing his hat, 'you are the only woman in the world.'

'Thank you, sir,' said she, and turned and passed on her way.

She was pained and humiliated more than she could have believed possible. Could an educated gentleman really descend to so low and shameless a condition as that? And through what? Suddenly—she knew not at the moment quite why—she thought of her father. Considering all she had heard and guessed, was it within the range of possibility that he could become such a poor creature as that she had parted from? The phrase 'the round earth over' still hung in her ear, and the turn of the man's voice; and she remembered what they reminded her of—her father's last letter, or, at least, the last letter of the man who represented himself as her father   She was struck stock-still an instant, and then she ran back to where she had left the man, and still on; but she did not find him. She returned, and passed out of the Park and home to her lodgings by Portman Square and Baker Street, with her thought cast forward to the meeting she had arranged for the following evening; would she then see the man she had encountered that night, or another?

She sat down to read to allay such thoughts, and she accomplished her end; but when she at length went to bed, very late, and with her brain made wakeful by the effort of her reading, her ugly and anxious thoughts returned upon her with redoubled force. If her father were really such an one as that man, or perhaps that very one, what should she do? She asked herself, 'What if she found he was that very man?' and she was appalled and ashamed to think that no affection would spring in her heart towards him, and that she would rather he were dead. But her father might not be like the man she had met, or at least not so wretched a creature as he—and then—then she prayed God that she might learn what duty and love would teach. When at length she dropped asleep, she conversed with men with Bardolphian countenances, who all somehow were her uncles; and after a period of tangled discussion with them and uncertainty about the colour of their eyes, she would start awake, and again think of her father.

Next day passed with her usual duties; and in the evening, after she had gone through and marked a pile of her pupils' exercises— she had been asked to go again to Rutland Gate, but she had excused herself—she set out to find Mrs. Ackland Snow's, Tobacconist, near the New North Road. She had discovered that the last delivery of letters in that region, as in her own, began about nine o'clock, and at that hour she intended to be at the door of Mrs. Ackland Snow. She had already looked at her map of London, and now she took the train to King's Cross, whence she rode by omnibus to her destination. It was scarcely dark, and she found without difficulty Nelson Street. It was a quiet street, of which she was glad ; and it contained only such two- or three-storeyed houses as are peculiar to certain quarters of London, and as appear always striving, but without conspicuous success, to look genteel. Such houses are commonly found to be let in tenements and to swarm with children—the one possession in which the poor are rich. The aspect of the houses, however, cheered Isabel's heart a little ; for she thought whoever lived there could not be absolutely sunk to the lowest ebb. She found the shop of ' Ackland Snow, Tobacconist,' but she did not enter at once ; she walked slowly up and down on the other side of the way, waiting for the postman to appear, while boys and girls loitering along the pavement with the supper beer wondered why a veiled lady, tall and grand-looking as a duchess, should be 'hanging about' their street. Isabel was beginning to find such notice somewhat embarrassing, when her attention was fixed by the approach of the postman. After a rat-tat here and there, he went to ' Ackland Snow's.' A bell tinkled as he opened the door, which plainly signified that little business was done, and that there was not always a person in attendance in the shop. Isabel crossed the street to enter, but she was no earlier than a man who hurried along the pavement with the aid of a stick, and whom, with some amazement, but no difficulty, she recognised as the man she had met the evening before. Seeing him, she drew back a little, and let him enter first. She therefore neither hindered his question nor was too late to catch it.

'Has that letter come for us to-night, Mrs. Snow?' he asked.

Mrs. Snow, a stout and comfortable-seeming person, handed him a letter without a word, and at the same moment Isabel stepped forward and put up her veil. The man looked, and his jaw dropped. He turned, took off his hat, set it on the counter, and sat down in a chair with gloomy and tragic resignation.

'Mrs. Snow,' said he, frowning and pursing his lips, 'I believe I have got them again!'

'Oh dear—oh dear!' said Mrs. Snow in a soothing tone. 'Don't say that, Mr. Doughty!'

'It grieves me to say it, Mrs. Snow,' said he, folding his arms, 'but I believe I have!'

'Please, Mr. Doughty, then,' said Mrs.

Snow, 'like a good man, which you are, don't go and 'ave 'em here.'

'Is your name "Doughty"?' asked Isabel; having heard the name twice, she was now pretty certain of its sound.

'She speaks!' he muttered aside, unfolding his arms and relaxing somewhat the ferocity of his aspect. 'It is—it must be she!' And he slowly turned his eyes on her and rose. 'Madam,' said he, 'I am the miserable individual baptismally named Alexander Doughty, at your service.'

'Let me ask you, then, Mr. Doughty,' said Isabel, 'how it is I find you receiving a letter addressed to Mr. Raynor?' And she pointed to the letter lying, face upward, on the counter.

'Mr. Raynor is his friend, ma'am,' said Mrs. Snow, 'as he fetches and carries for, and as he has been that kind to, nobody knows!'

'A truce to compliments, Mrs. Snow,'

said Mr. Doughty. ' You are trenching on my private affairs ; you should not do it, Mrs. Snow ; you must not.' Then, turning to Isabel, he said : 'I am a journalist, madam, and Mr. Raynor is my chief.'

'I wish to see Mr. Raynor,' said Isabel. ' Will you take me to him ? '

' Your desire to see the chief, madam,' said Mr. Doughty, ' is natural, and even laudable, but——' And Mr. Doughty for once seemed at a loss for a word.

' You wonder,' said Isabel, ' why I should wish to see him ; that letter to him is from me—I am Isabel Raynor.'

' Land of Goshen ! ' exclaimed Doughty. ' The only woman in the world is Miss Raynor, and I never guessed it ! Let us withdraw, Miss Raynor, and speak of this. I perceive an explanation is due to you.' Then, as he approached the door, he turned and said to her in a low voice : 'I must tell you he does not know of this.—Good-night, Mrs Snow,' he said aloud, as he held the door open.

Isabel passed out, and he followed her, buttoning up his frock-coat.

CHAPTER XI

MR. DOUGHTY EXPLAINS

'Which way?' asked Isabel, when both she and Mr. Alexander Doughty were on the pavement.

'Let us,' said Mr. Doughty, turning his back on the New North Road, 'walk in this direction, Miss Raynor;' and he was politely careful to take the outer side of the pavement. 'This,' he continued, 'will be quieter for our purpose.'

'But,' asked Isabel, stopping short, 'is it not in this direction that you live?'

'It is,' said Mr. Doughty, with solemn emphasis. 'But you shall hear, if you will permit me to explain;' and they went on again. 'Your father and myself had rooms some time ago in the house of Mrs. Ackland Snow. She is an excellent woman, but rather fidgety; and her fidgets and the odour of her Irish twist, brown shag, and penny Pickwicks were too much for your father's shattered nerves. It is possible that you do not know that your father's nerves *are* shattered; they are not shattered in exactly the way mine are, but they are *shattered*.'

'Will you be so good, Mr. Doughty,' said Isabel, 'as explain to me, as you promised, the character of your connection with my father?'

She said that somewhat curtly, and then felt a little ashamed of her curtness; for the forces of attraction and repulsion were striving within her: she was drawn to think kindly and gratefully of Mr. Doughty, because—she had understood from Mrs. Snow's words—he had been a faithful friend to her father; and

yet, when she looked at the shaking Bardolphian creature beside her and thought of
his abject behaviour of the evening before,
she suspected that he might have had to do
with her father's declension, and dislike and
disgust swayed her for the moment.

'Your father and myself, Miss Raynor,'
said Mr. Doughty, 'are bound together in a
friendship of considerable standing. A good
many years ago—indeed, I may say, when
you were an infant in your mother's arms—I
was your father's sub.'

'His what?'

'His "sub."; which is, I may explain, an
abbreviation used among men of the press for
sub-editor. I was his sub.,' he repeated, as if he
enjoyed the word, 'on the "Weekly Bulletin,"
and we worked together with the extremest
harmony; and the harmony arose, I may
say, from kindness on his side and good-will
on my own. I admired your father, Miss

Raynor. He was a man—and he is,' said he, half-aside, and as if to some one who was likely to deny it—'of brilliant abilities, all of which were squandered in editorial and journalistic drudgery for an unenlightened public. I wrote, if you will permit me to say so, with a pen dipped in common ink ——'

'And whisky,' thought Isabel; but she refrained from hurting Mr. Doughty's feelings by saying it.

'——he,' continued Mr. Doughty, 'wrote with a pen steeped in a finer fluid. Moreover, he was the best company in the world—at least in the whole range of Fleet Street; and for that matter he is still; yes, he is still—occasionally.'

'You mean, I suppose,' said Isabel bitterly, 'when he is in a condition in which I would not like to see him ?'

'Miss Raynor,' said Mr. Doughty weightily, and he stopped to add emphasis to his words, 'you are under a grave misapprehension. If my meaning had been as you have conceived it, I should not have alluded to the matter in conversation with a lady.' And Mr. Doughty walked on again. 'No,' he continued, 'the meaning you suggested would apply, perchance, to the miserable individual now walking by your side, but it would *not* apply to the chief. I may be—I believe I am—good company only when I have achieved some refreshment ; for instance, I am not myself to-night, I beg to assure you ; but it is not so with the chief. We both have our foibles, our weaknesses—our vices, if you will,' he added in a ferocity of criticism of ' self and friend,' ' but, as I ventured to observe a moment ago, they are not alike—I have mine ; the chief has his.'

Up to that point Isabel had held herself in ; she had hoped that by patiently listening to Mr. Alexander Doughty, she would arrive quickly at an understanding of the relations between him and her father, and of the condition in which her father was living; but now, between impatience with his sonorous maunderings and a strange acute feeling of jealousy that this man—whom she could not but despise, strive how she might after a better feeling for him—that this man knew all about her father, and thought it necessary to defend him against the misunderstandings of his ignorant daughter, she let herself go.

'It is a strange, an unnatural thing,' she broke forth, 'that I should be gathering all the knowledge I have of my father from a— a person whom I have met in the most casual way——'

'And that, you would say, Miss Raynor,' interrupted Mr. Doughty, 'not under the most favourable circumstances.'

'Certainly,' said she—for she could not spare him now—'not under the most favourable circumstances. But that I have been ignorant of my father, or of his condition, is not my fault. It is his own—or yours, who have come between us. When he first wrote to me, three years ago, why did he refuse to see me? Was it you that persuaded him to that?'

'I, Miss Raynor?' exclaimed Mr. Doughty stopping again—this time in the sheerest amazement. 'God forbid! You little know, Miss Raynor—you totally misunderstand me;' and his hands began to tremble as he clasped them on the head of his stick. 'I would spend my last shilling with your father; I *have* spent it oftener than once! I would give my last drop of blood—such as it is—to serve him! *I* come between you? *I* persuade him not to see his own daughter—and such a daughter? You little know!'

'Forgive me,' said she in an impulse of self-reproach when she saw his distress. 'No doubt I have wrongly accused you.   But how can I understand if you will not explain ?   Do not tell me any more about my father's life—he can tell me that himself; but tell me, as you promised, how you come to be receiving letters intended for him, and what you meant by saying he knew nothing of it ?'

'Miss Raynor,' said Mr. Doughty, 'bear with me an instant, and I will tell you succinctly.   It was I that saw the announcement in the papers of your appointment as mistress in the college for ladies.   I showed it to your father and begged him, almost on my knees, to make himself known to you ; but he refused absolutely to do so, for reasons which he thought sufficient, but which I ventured to consider inadequate.   Your father's situation was at that particular moment desperate ; our uncle—ahem !—well, Miss Raynor, it was desperate beyond anything you can dream of desperation.'

' Perhaps,' said Isabel, ' I can dream more in accordance with reality than you imagine.'

' At any rate, Miss Raynor, to understand how I came to do what I am about to relate to you that I did, you must know that I had for years been accustomed to act, if I may be allowed the comparison, as jackal to the lion, and that it had become necessary for me to assume the entire control of our joint affairs, your father's and my own, financial and other. I would relate to you how that had become necessary, but you have signified to me that it would not be agreeable.'

' Not now, please,' said Isabel; ' go on merely with your explanation.'

' Very good, Miss Raynor,' said Mr. Doughty. ' When we were in a tight place— that is to say, when we found ourselves in straitened circumstances——'

' In short, when you were hard up.'

'——in short, when we were hard up, it

was I who had to find relief from our embarrassment: it devolved upon me to find replenishment for the exchequer.'

'Do you mean,' asked Isabel coldly, 'in plain words, that you have had to keep my father?'

'Not at all. Do not misunderstand me, I pray. I am not uttering complaint; I am but stating a fact. And I ask you to remember that I said I was jackal to the lion. It therefore fell upon me, when provision for our wants was required, to go the round to find occupation for the refined pen of your father, or, failing that, for my own rude quill.'

'And if both of these failed?' asked Isabel, in sure expectation of the answer.

'Then,' said Mr. Doughty, 'I would try to find temporary accommodation from a friend. Both these resources failed us at the time I spoke of.'

'Now I understand completely,' said Isabel. 'The jackal had one trick—one resource—more than the lion.

'I ventured to suggest to your father——'

'I understand,' interrupted Isabel. 'You suggested to my father that he should apply to me for help, and he would not hear of it; he said he was not yet fallen so low as to ask his daughter—a girl only beginning life for herself—for such help as his weakness or his wickedness would not allow him to provide for himself. Was not that what he said?' she demanded eagerly.

'Miss Raynor,' said Mr. Doughty, 'you are as clever as you are charming. He spoke much to that effect.'

'Mr. Doughty,' said Isabel, 'I shall be obliged to you exceedingly if you will not pay me compliments.—You, however, had not the same view as my father, your old chief. You therefore wrote to me in his name, telling him nothing of it.'

'What first made me think of it was, that my handwriting was not unlike your father's.'

'And you received from me a certain sum of money, which I had sent as to my father.'

'And which, Miss Raynor,' said Mr. Doughty, 'I religiously expended on your father, and on him alone.'

'Oh, that is not a point we need discuss. The jackal, I suppose, is worthy of his hire.'

'Miss Raynor,' said Mr. Doughty with palpable emotion—he had stopped again and faced her, with his hands clasped on his stick—'you should not say that. It is unworthy of you to stab so cruelly one who has learnt to admire your generous qualities, even though that one is the miserable, broken individual before you. You should not—you should not, really.' His lip trembled with emotion, and a tear sprang in his eye, which he ferociously flicked away with his finger. 'If there is one person in the world whom I care for besides the chief, it is yourself; and I expect you to believe me when I say that whenever I have applied to you it has been only on your father's account, and that whatever you have bestowed in answer to my applications has been strictly expended on your father to the uttermost farthing.'

'I believe you,' said Isabel, impulsively giving him her hand. 'Forgive me.'

She was so sorry for the pain she had evidently given the poor creature, and she so saw him touched with a pathetic dignity, that a new revulsion of feeling came upon her in which she could almost have kissed him to assuage the pain she had caused. But the trembling and spasmodic fervour with which he grasped her proffered hand drove back all such inclination.

'Are we not nearly there yet?' she asked, going on again.

'To tell you the simple truth, Miss Raynor,' said Mr. Doughty, now less constrained and more cheerful, 'your father is not in our rooms.'

Isabel stopped at once. 'Where is he, then?' she asked.

'At this precise moment he is waiting in a certain house in a lane off the Ratcliff Highway for his bill to be paid.'

'Bill?—for what? Not—not for drink?' asked Isabel with a new horror upon her.

'No, Miss Raynor, not for drink. That is not the form the chief's refreshment takes.'

'What is it, then?' demanded Isabel. 'Tell me the truth. I hope I am not afraid or ashamed to hear what you may have to say.'

'Well, Miss Raynor, in a word, the devil that has tempted him and brought him to his present pass is opium. I have seen its damnable method of working—excuse my strong epithet—from its initial stage. He began to smoke opium from an innocent and laudable motive—nothing less, indeed, than to find " copy " to be sold for what it would bring in the Magazine market, to furnish forth the expenses attendant on your birth. He visited an opium den of the East End, in the days when both opium dens and the East End properly so called were much more dangerous places to enter than they are now. He went there by himself, and some time later he piloted no less a person than Charles Dickens thither. I am declaring to you the simple truth. But he did not make a habit of smoking the seductive drug until your poor mother's death. Then he was distracted, and could find no comfort in anything, and forgetfulness, only in his opium sleep.—My dear Miss Raynor, let the rest be silence.'

'Mr. Doughty,' exclaimed Isabel, without a moment's hesitation, 'let us go at once and pay his bill and get him out of the dreadful place!'

'My dear young lady,' said Mr. Doughty, 'I should say "agreed" with the utmost alacrity, were it not that my purse is absolutely empty. To say truth,' added he, with an attempt to laugh which sounded rusty and unused, 'I had looked forward to a remittance from you to-night to release him.'

'Come,' said she hurriedly. 'Which way must we go? I have money.'

Mr. Doughty set his face towards the New North Road. Isabel swept along the pavement at a pace which somewhat taxed Mr. Doughty's rheumatic limbs to maintain.

'We must take a cab,' said he. 'And will it not be best for me to go alone? It is a dangerous region for a young lady to venture into, more particularly at this time of night.'

' A cab by all means,' said Isabel ; ' but I shall go with you ; I am not afraid.'

' It is,' said he, ' for you to ordain, Miss Raynor, and for me to obey. It must be a four-wheeler then.'

They hurried on in silence till they had passed Mrs. Ackland Snow's again, and were nearing the New North Road.

' He goes off, I suppose,' said Isabel, ' at intervals to this place, and remains there till you find him and release him ? '

' Exactly so,' said Mr. Doughty.

' How long has he been gone this time ? ' asked she.

' Three days,' answered he.

' Three days ! I should have thought that was enough to kill a man ! Dreadful ! Dreadful ! Let us make haste ! '

When they reached the New North Road,

Mr. Doughty produced from his waistcoat pocket a whistle, and blew a call, which was speedily answered by the appearance of a four-wheeler. He opened the door, and when Isabel had entered the cab he closed it again.

'But are you not coming?' she asked.

'I am coming, certainly,' answered Mr. Doughty. 'But my place is with the driver on the box.'

'I cannot hear of such a thing,' said Isabel. 'You will catch cold; you are not wrapt up.'

'I am quite sufficiently clothed, thank you, Miss Raynor; and I would prefer, if you will permit me, to sit on the box and smoke a pipe.'

Thus it came to pass that Isabel did not hear what instructions were given to the driver; and they drove away, on and on, through regions to her altogether unknown.

She remembered, however, that Mr. Doughty had said that the opium den was near the Ratcliff Highway, and she was familiar enough with her map of London to know the direction they must take. They passed down the New North Road, and presently they left the bustle and the glare behind, and rolled through darkness and comparative silence, with large, comfortable-seeming houses on either hand, where in the past had dwelt substantial men from the City, whose descendants or successors have gone farther afield; over the dark and gruesome canal, with evil-smelling chemical works on the one hand and tall square piles of sweet-smelling wood on the other; on, again, through the darkness, picked out here and there at wide intervals with tall and despondent gas-lamps, and out again into clamour and bustle, blazing gas in shops and gin palaces, and flaring naphtha on the stalls; and then out into what was plainly a great thoroughfare and past an imposing church, withdrawn deep into the shadows at the junction of two ways, and looking serenely and pityingly down on the surging tides of human life, business and pleasure, sin and sorrow, that met about its gates ; on and still on.

During this progress, with the deafening rattle of the wheels and of the slung windows in her ears, Isabel passed into a semi-conscious state. She knew she was wearing farther and farther east ; she saw how different were the scenes she was passing through from those to which she was accustomed in the neighbourhood of her lodgings, a good many miles behind her ; and she wondered anew at the vast, the mysterious, London in which she dwelt. She was a tolerably learned young lady, and she was able to compare in her mind the great capitals of the world—to compare, at least, what she had read of those in the past with what she knew of this in the present—and she said to herself that, though Rome was great, and Babylon was great, and Nineveh, and Thebes, yet London was greater far by reason, not of fine buildings and a general impression of magnificence and imposing outward show, but of its vastness and its swarm of men and women, each in an orderly way doing that which is right in his own eyes, none daring to make him afraid. The wonder of London, she felt, is its people. Then she went on to think particularly of her father—a weak unit swimming, floating hither and thither, in this sea of humanity. Now that she was definitely set out to find him, her anxiety concerning him and her horror of his situation had changed into a kind of gentle, romantic expectation. She had read of De Quincey, Coleridge, and other confirmed consumers of opium, and the glamour of these names made her father's fault appear less a vice than an amiable and poetic weakness.

She was rudely awakened out of these dreams by the stoppage of the cab and the appearance of Mr. Doughty at the door. He said it was necessary to descend there and to walk a little way. She descended, and walked along the pavement by his side—not without a tremor or two, for dark, foreign, and wild-looking men—browned and baked with wind and sun—stared curiously at her as she passed. They came to the corner of a dark and noisome alley, which they were about to turn down, when they were accosted by a policeman. He looked hard at Mr. Doughty.

'Oh,' said he, 'it's you, is it, sir? Your chief down there again, I suppose. Is the lady going down with you?'

'Yes, policeman,' said Mr. Doughty, in his profoundest tones, 'the lady thinks it necessary to go with me—she thinks it absolutely necessary.'

'In that case, ma'am—or miss,' said the policeman—'I must go down with you—only to see that no harm comes to you ; for they're a queer lot down there.'

CHAPTER XII

A PRODIGAL FATHER

Down the noisome lane, or alley, Isabel and
Mr. Doughty passed in the rear of the policeman. It was so narrow and so dark that
they thought it well to keep in the middle of
the way; and yet they scarce avoided contact
with dingy figures that flitted past them in
and out of gaping doorways, and with
children that squalled and scrambled in the
gutters; for in that dreadful region night and
day were confounded even for the youngest.
At the end of the alley was a dark little
square, and to a tumble-down house at the
farther side the policeman led, and they followed. The doorway was below the level of

the street, and was approached by a flight of half-a-dozen steps, worn very much away by the tread and scuffle of countless feet. Into this den or cave they descended; and now at a suggestion Isabel would have turned back, for these squalid surroundings had dis pelled the romance of opium-smoking, and the horrid expectation of what she might see oppressed and terrified her. But neither of her companions said a word, and she went on with them as if without hesitation—on to a door on one side of the dark passage, above which hung a small paraffin lamp, smoking and stinking. The policeman lifted the latch and opened the door, and then stood aside for the others to enter. Isabel drew back.

'I think,' said she, 'I will wait here.'

'I will go in,' said Mr. Doughty, 'and find him, and discover what there is to pay.'

He entered, and Isabel and the policeman remained together by the door. They had a full view of the long, low room, the atmosphere of which was thick with the brown and sickly opium smoke. A heavy silence prevailed, but yet Isabel was instinctively aware that there were many men in the awful place. No lamp illumined the gloom—nothing save a lurid glow proceeding from a raised brazier of charcoal at the farther end, and points of light here and there, which were alternately bright and dull, and which, when bright, made little halos in the dense, smoky atmosphere. As her eyes became used to the peculiar gloom she made out wooden bunks, ranged above each other against the wall, like the berths of a ship, and in the bunks she dimly descried strange figures disposed fantastically as on beds of languid torture. Now and then she heard murmurs of uncouth speech, which rose heavily from the silence, and slowly sank back into silence again.

Meanwhile, Mr. Doughty had made his way

down the den. He was met mid-way by a
bowing and gesticulating Chinaman, to whom
he seemed to explain his purpose, and with
whom he moved towards the brazier. There
they stopped, looming large and shadowy
against it; after a moment or two the Chinaman returned alone down the room. Then it
seemed to Isabel as if a face sprang out of the
darkness around the brazier. Close against it,
steeped in the glow of the charcoal, she saw
the grizzled head of a man with thin nose and
lank, close-shaven jaw. The man sat with his
chin in his hands, gazing into the fire; but
presently he raised his head with his face half-
turned towards the door to look at Mr.
Doughty, who stood on the other side of the
brazier, and then Isabel's heart rose and sank,
for she was sure she saw her father. At that
moment the Chinaman appeared through the
haze immediately before her. He bowed, and
he smiled with an expansive, all-embracing

friendliness; but there was an expression in his slanting eyes which made Isabel shudder.

'It is my own fault,' she said to herself; 'I should not have come here.'

The policeman, however, came to her relief. 'Quick, Johnny, quick,' said he; and the Chinaman turned away, smiling and bowing still, and moved noiselessly back to the brazier.

In a moment or two Mr. Doughty came back, and said the Chinaman's demand was for so much—naming a sum which seemed extravagant even for three days' unremitting consumption of his seductive poison—but that, with Miss Raynor's permission, he would give him so much less.

'Give him what he asks for,' said Isabel, putting her purse into Mr. Doughty's hand, 'and let us get away.'

Mr. Doughty's look of mingled surprise and conscious worth at having untold money entrusted to him was good to see. 'I will accomplish,' said he, 'the business with expedition.'

He hurried away; and soon returned, leading by the arm a lean, haggard man with hair and dress disordered and creased, pale with the pasty pallor of the Chinaman, loose-lipped, and with every nerve twitching in reaction from the prolonged effect of the drug. He seemed but half-conscious, and he walked sadly and shamblingly, with his eyes on the ground.

Isabel leaned back, as if she would faint, against the door-post. She experienced such bitter disappointment and piercing of heart as she had never before known. Was this pitiable creature her father—whom she had dreamed of comforting and cheering, and upon whom she had been ready to pour out all her affection? Did he know that his daughter was there, waiting for him—the girl whom he had let slip from care and ken for more than twenty years? Perhaps he did not yet know, nor fully comprehend. She found herself thinking it would be well that it should be so. She shrank from embracing, even from touching him. She was filled with shame for him, and yet she was ashamed of her shame.

In this turbulent state of emotion she scarcely noticed that he was being hurried up the lane, by Mr. Doughty on one side and the policeman on the other, and that she herself was hasting after them, away from that hideous Inferno, whose stifling fumes seemed still creeping and writhing about her.

They found the cab waiting for them where they had left it. Mr. Doughty opened the door and helped his chief to enter. Then he turned to Miss Raynor. 'Miss Raynor,' said he, in a low but impressive voice, 'you see him at his worst—his very worst; you must not judge of him as you see him now.'

'No,' said she, stung somewhat with her former jealousy that a stranger should know more of her father than she knew; 'I must not—I do not. You have my purse, Mr. Doughty; will you give the policeman something for his kindness?' Then turning to the policeman she said, 'Thank you very much,' and entered the cab, and sat down opposite her father.

Mr. Doughty did as she requested. Then, closing the cab-door without a word, he mounted again beside the driver. Isabel felt curiously grateful for so small a matter, and was in some sense cheered by it. She was compelled to see that those delicate turns of behaviour which are taken to mark a gentleman were still possible even to so poor and soddened a creature as Mr. Doughty, and she therefore was inclined to be hopeful about her father. Moreover, she considered and said to herself: 'There must, after all, be something good and attractive about him even for poor Mr. Doughty to have remained an attached and faithful friend these many years.' All which is significant evidence of the prostrate condition to which her feelings and hopes had been reduced by the sight of her father.

They had not driven very far—Isabel on one seat and her father leaning back in the corner of the other—and she was wondering whether he was not asleep, when he suddenly threw himself forward, with his face in his hands and his elbows resting on his knees, and sobbed aloud. Upon that the imprisoned founts of feeling in Isabel's generous breast burst forth and swept away all doubt and speculation ; she became simply a large-hearted woman and a daughter aware that there before her was a man, her father, needing pity and consolation.

'Father!' she cried, and sank on her knees before him. 'Don't! Don't! I'm here!' She took one of his hands, which he yielded to her, and she put her arm about him.

'Rise, rise!' he said in a sharp treble of agony. 'It is I should be there!'

She yielded to his insistent hand, and sat beside him.

'Don't speak to me,' said he; 'let me look at you. You are like your mother— poor mother!—but stronger—much stronger. How does it happen?'

Isabel looked at him, and for the first time met his eye: there was a light in it which belied the haggard debauchery of the countenance, and which at once made her feel that she was not the chief person there. She was relieved and soothed; she was now certain that her father was not a soddened brute;

that, much and terribly though he might have tried, tortured, and debased his body, his intellect and soul still shone clear through all. He leaned back again, looking at her and dreaming, and she sat content (comparatively), and still held his hand, in spite of its nervous twitching, pleased to find it warm and of a beautiful shape. They said no further word to each other till the cab stopped and Mr. Doughty came to the door. This time it was Isabel that helped her father. He took her arm out of the cab and into the lodging, which was on the ground-floor of one of the houses of Norfolk Street.

Seeing that Mr. Doughty had not followed them in, and hearing voices without for some instants in tolerably loud debate, Isabel—who feared the cabman was in process of being dismissed, and who, moreover, now felt herself responsible for her father and his friend—went to the door.

'I had intended,' she heard Mr. Doughty say in portentous tones to the cabman—'I had intended to bestow upon you a considerable honorarium ; but, considering the suggestions you have rudely urged concerning this adorable and angelic young lady, I shall not bestow it.'

' But, at least, sir,' said the cabman—who was evidently very civil, as cabmen go—'I hope you won't go and forget the half-pint of Scotch I got.'

' Hush ! ' said Mr. Doughty. ' I will not.'

' Mr. Doughty,' called she, ' don't send the cab away ; I shall want it to take me home presently. Ask the cabman to wait, please.'

' All right, miss,' the cabman answered for himself.

Isabel was returning to her father, when she heard the voice of Mr. Doughty calling her. She waited ; and he came to her with business-like air.

'One moment, Miss Raynor,' said he. 'I beg to resign the trust you confided to me'—and he handed back her purse. 'The disbursements—of which I have made a note on this morsel of paper—cover Johnny Chinaman's charges and the cab fare up till now, together with a shilling which I ventured to borrow to furnish some slight refreshment for the cabman and myself. Did I do wrong?'

'Oh no,' said Isabel; and she secretly thought well of him for his confession that he had 'borrowed.' 'But,' she added, 'you must take charge of a little money for my father. He ought, by the way, to eat something at once. I suppose he has not had much food at the Chinaman's these three days?'

'Food, Miss Raynor?' said Mr. Doughty. 'The only food supplied or demanded in that Hades is opium! And the chief would not taste solid food at present if he had it.'

'And the shops are all closed!' she exclaimed. She was thinking that she might have bought some soup for him; but nothing could be done now; and she reflected that, after all, he was probably no worse off than he had been many a time before after he had been sated with his drug. It was inevitable he should wait for her provision, but she would ensure that his wants should be properly supplied next day. 'I suppose,' said she, 'that you have nothing in the house that could be easily got ready?'

'I do not know, Miss Raynor,' said Mr. Doughty; 'but I am tolerably sure there is not. Food, Miss Raynor, is not our strong point in this house.'

'I suspected as much. But,' said she, with good sense, 'it is with neglecting your food that you foolish men confirm your dreadful habits.'

'You are right, Miss Raynor. We weak male mortals go completely wrong when we have not the clear head and the strong heart of the better sex with us.'

'Compliments again, Mr. Doughty!' said Isabel.

'Simple truth, I assure you,' said Mr. Doughty. 'And now, Miss Raynor, will you permit me to say that I think it wise of you not to propose to hold much conversation with your father now. Apart from the fact that it is very nearly midnight, the chief is at this present time in his very lowest condition. I would offer to escort you to your—ahem—abode, but I do not think it would be well to leave the chief alone as he is.'

'What?' said Isabel. 'He would not try, surely, to go back to that dreadful place?'

'No,' said Mr. Doughty; 'not that. But he might try to lay violent hands on himself.—But pray, do not be alarmed. I know his ways, and I will look after him. He sleeps little, but I sleep less, and on these particular occasions I keep a special watch upon him.'

Isabel hesitated ; for these words of Mr. Doughty brought back doubts and fears. Ought she to stay with her father—to soothe and strengthen him, if so be she might ? It was characteristic of her frank independence and her lack of self-consciousness not to view this at all as a question of propriety with regard to herself. She entered the little sitting-room, determined to let herself be decided by what her father might chance to say. He was reclining limp in an easy-chair —the comfortless, casterless easy-chair of the London lodging-house—apparently in a state of apathy. His eyes found her, however, as soon as she entered.

' Don't take your things off,' said he—she was only undoing a button or two of her jacket. 'You must not stay here ; this place is not fit for you.'

'I will go,' said Mr. Doughty, 'and interview our landlady;' and he discreetly withdrew.

'I do not propose to stay, father,' said Isabel, going nearer to him. 'I have lodgings of my own.'

'Don't come near me at present, my child,' said he. 'Sit there, and let me look at you. I am glad you have rooms of your own— but not in this house, I hope—not in this house. It is a dreadful house.' He kept his eyes sadly and wistfully fixed on her. 'You have come to me as an angel of God, my dear. I do not ask you now how you found me : we will talk of that and other things by-and-by. I cannot talk of anything now ; I— I am not well enough.'

'Promise me, father,' said she, leaning towards him, 'that you will take some food at once.'

'Food ? I need no food now, my child.

It is meat and drink to look on you. I have often longed to see you—to see how the poor baby that they took from me was grown.'

'My poor father!' she cried, and before he could hinder her, she was on her knees beside him.

'And you are my daughter!' said he, still gazing at her wistfully and half-absently. 'You are very beautiful, my dear—far more beautiful than I could have imagined you to be.'

'Don't say these things, father,' said Isabel blushing, but pleased.

'It is a good thing to be beautiful, and it is good to know it. The chances are that a truly beautiful woman has a beautiful nature; there is no kind of doubt of that with you.' Then he let his chin drop on his breast and fixed his eyes on vacancy as he murmured:

> ' I remember one that perished; sweetly did she speak
>   and move ;
> Such an one do I remember—

I cannot talk now; I am tired; I am not quite well.' He roused himself a little and said: 'Come and see me to-morrow if you can. Yes; come, and I'll talk with you.'

His chin dropped again on his breast and his eyes closed. He seemed to slide away into sleep; and after a minute or two Isabel rose and quietly went out. She found Mr. Doughty waiting at the outer door to see her into her cab. She told him she would visit her father early next evening, gave him a kindly adieu, and was driven away as the clocks of Islington reproachfully tolled her out the hour of twelve.

CHAPTER XIII

SAHIB GEORGE

WHILE Isabel was thus occupied with the discovery of her father, the two young men down in Lancashire, whose hearts she had set aflutter and aflame—her cousin George and Alan Ainsworth—had begun to apply themselves, each in his way, to the task of winning her. Ainsworth, on his part, had exerted himself to find a post in London, and had succeeded with a celerity that surprised him, at the same time that it flattered his vanity; for he could not but think that his own deserts had much to do with his quick success. He did not then know, nor guess—though, when he did know, he was properly humbled and chastened in spirit—that the chief whose service he was leaving, who was one of the best of men and editors, had really bespoken for him the place for which he had applied on the 'Evening Banner.' All he was aware of in the excitement of the occasion was that the 'Banner' wanted him in London at once, and that his chief had generously agreed to let him go.

George Suffield, on the other hand, had resolved upon a course which the committal of all the Suffield business into his hands left him free to choose. He had the self-confidence and the stout grain characteristic of so many Englishmen, which bear their possessors bravely through supreme difficulties of war, administration, and trade, but which cause them to blunder egregiously in the delicate business of love. George did not hesitate for a moment to believe that he would prevail on Isabel to be his wife, that his desire and his

will must overbear all her scruples and doubts;
he therefore wasted no time in vague long-
ings, in downcast speculations as to ways and
means of making himself more agreeable to
her—he meant to marry her, to keep loyally
his promise not to trouble her with his ad-
dresses for a time, and meanwhile to prepare
such a position for her as could not fail to fill
her and himself with joy and pride. The
Suffield business was big, but he would make
it bigger. The dear old dad—bless him!—
had prospered exceedingly in the good old
jog-trot ways; but his son was born into a
sharper, adroiter—perhaps less scrupulous—
time, when a fortune might be made at a
stroke, and he was resolved to lose no advantage which the turning of the wheel of trade
might offer him.

It chanced that Fate—or the Devil—had
just then placed at his elbow a subtle, insinua-
tive adviser to tempt him into risky ways—

an unusual adviser—an unlikely adviser, many might think—but all the more dangerous a tempter for his being unusual and unlikely. Daniel Trichinopoly had been taken into the service of the firm, apparently; in reality, he was attached to the person of young Mr. Suffield, much as he had been to that of the Sahib Raynor. There was nothing of the firm's usual business to which he could be set, but he lightly and easily slipped into the place of personal attendant and deferential and confidential retainer to the Sahib George. And George was more than pleased. He was of a generous and magnificent nature; it did not trouble him that Daniel did little or nothing to earn the emolument conferred on him; it was enough—indeed, more than enough— that he flattered him by his subservience and added to his feeling of consequence by his dark and inferior presence. Daniel put on a lavish show of obsequious admiration and affection, and George patronised and protected him. George suggested that since Daniel was to go in and out with him among the throngs of men, it would be well if he dressed more in the English mode—he would give him wherewithal to array himself properly—and Daniel humbly crossed his dark hands on his white, guileless bosom, and professed the extremest desire to please a master who was great and good, strong and beautiful—the heavens, said Daniel, were wide, but they were not wider than the beneficence of the Sahib George. So Daniel dressed himself in English attire—dark trousers and a loose alpaca coat—all except his head, on which he still wore the blameless turban, and was thenceforward assiduous in his service and in his flattery. He looked after the clothes of the Sahib George; he waited upon the Sahib George at table and cooked rare little dishes for him; he fetched and carried for the Sahib

George, and, like a faithful dog, was always found at heel when wanted either in the house or in the works or in the office in town; and constantly he dropped the insidious word in season into the Sahib George's ear. George had a vast opinion of his own shrewdness and judgment, but in reality he had much of his father's simplicity. He had a kind of large, open contempt for Daniel, and he would have been amazed and indignant if an acute observer had hinted that his black henchman was beginning to exert a prodigious influence over him; yet the extent of Daniel's influence, even in the first week of his service, may be judged from the following.

There had been supplied to the Suffield mills by a Liverpool broker sundry bales of American cotton which, when opened, made George swear, not loud but deep; not only was the cotton of inferior quality, but the weight was made up by stones and other foreign rubbish packed in the midst of the bales. He exclaimed, in the hearing of Daniel, against the villainy of American shippers and Liverpool brokers both.

' With regard, Sahib George,' said Daniel, in his childlike humility, ' why the Sahibs of the great English mills do they use much-much Amelican cotton? I beg to try to understand, but the same time I must say I am not able. I have think very much, but— no—it is not for the scarcity of fine and pure cotton stuff non-procurable. The native coolie of India, my own people—oh yes!— they grow much-much cotton. With regard, Sahib, why the English Sahibs buy they not very much the cotton of their own great India? I beg to understand.'

George answered carelessly that not very much Indian cotton came into the market, and that what did was short and dirty—the fact was, he knew very little about it.

'With regard, Sahib,' asked the simple Daniel, 'do he also have big stones in the middle of him? I beg to understand.'

George did not know. But the effect of Daniel's words was that George resolved to inquire concerning Indian cotton the next time he visited Liverpool, and that was after two or three days.

It was thus that George Suffield set out upon his independent and aspiring course; and he was in that mood when Ainsworth chanced to meet him on the very last day of his Lancashire sojourn. Ainsworth had said farewell to the 'Lancashire Gazette' in the morning, betimes, and had arranged to travel to London by a late train, intending to spend the interval with a college friend who was a journalist in Liverpool. He was thus in Liverpool in his friend's company at the hour of lunch. His friend proposed to entertain him at a club whither resorted at luncheon-

time many representatives of Liverpool commerce—Liverpool shippers and Liverpool
brokers, especially brokers. When they
entered the dining-room of the club, Ainsworth discovered George Suffield occupied
at one of the tables with three or four men.
George did not see him, and he, remembering
how they had parted at Whitsuntide, made
no show of acquaintance with George. When
they had withdrawn to the smoking-room,
however, a hand was laid on Ainsworth's
shoulder, and a cheery voice spoke in his
ear—the hand and the voice of George
Suffield.

'Who would have thought of meeting
you here, Ainsworth?' he exclaimed. 'Not
that you haven't as much business to be here
as anyone else, but I should have thought
you'd be occupied with your paper at this
time of day.'

Ainsworth introduced him to his companion, and said that he was done with the 'Lancashire Gazette,' and was going to London that very night.

'Oh, indeed!' exclaimed George. 'You must come and dine with me—that is, if you have nothing better to do.'

Ainsworth answered that he doubted whether he could wait in Lancashire for dinner; he intended to travel late, but not so late as to preclude his reaching London and a hotel before midnight. While he spoke, he noted that George Suffield's eye wandered to a centre table, on which stood a rough deal box, and about which members of the club kept coming and going more and more with a subdued hum of talk and occasional bursts of laughter.

'What is going on there?' asked Ainsworth, looking from George to his friend.

His friend answered that he did not know, and rose to look.

'It's something of mine,' said George, with a conscious blush. 'I put it there. It's merely a joke; but I wish to show them—the cotton brokers, I mean—that that kind of thing shouldn't be allowed to happen too often. By Jingo!' he said, 'somebody's writing on the box!'

Somebody *was* writing in large chalk letters on the side of the open box—writing something which made those who read it shout with laughter.

'Let's see what it is,' said George, going to the table.

Ainsworth went with him, meeting his friend, who laughed, and said: 'It's not a bad joke.' This is what Ainsworth saw: in what appeared to be a large starch-box was a big stone, on which was pasted a written label—'Specimen of Messrs. Jones's middlings;' and on the box itself had just been written in chalk—'Specimen of Messrs. Suffield's size-box.' Ainsworth was sufficiently acquainted with the terms of Lancashire trade and manufacture to know that 'middlings' meant bale-cotton of average good quality; and that 'size' was the stuff with which manufacturers liberally dressed their webs to give their cotton cloths and calicoes more apparent substance. So he understood, and laughed; George Suffield had got *quid pro quo*, a Roland for his Oliver.

'So this is your joke, is it, Suffield?' said a little man coming and looking grimly on the small boulder.

'Yes, Jones,' said George. 'And this'— pointing to the chalk writing—'may be considered your joke; it has been made for you. So we're quits.'

Mr. Jones smiled wryly, but he said nothing; and George returned and sat down with Ainsworth.

'They laugh,' observed George in confidence, 'but they don't like it : I can see they don't. Of course, I know it's not they that put stones and old iron and rubbish in the bales to make weight ; but they are responsible ; they should keep their shippers in order. No ; I can see they don't like it. But that doesn't matter. I can do without them better than they can do without me. I can ship my own cotton if I like ; and I will !—And you are going to London to-night, Ainsworth ? I wish you could stay and dine with me.'

Thus he continued, trying to show interest in Ainsworth, but continuing to be excited and occupied with the effect of his joke practical on the cotton brokers. Presently there appeared on the opposite side of the street, looking up at the window where they sat, a black man in a white turban. Ainsworth noticed him first.

'Is not that,' said he to George, 'the black fellow that was Mr. Raynor's servant? I suppose he is in your service now—he is looking as if he wished to attract your attention.'

Daniel was in fact smiling, and smiling with a gentle inclination of the head.

'Yes,' said George; 'that's Daniel. He is my servant now; a useful, faithful creature,' said he with a pointed smile, which obviously meant: You suspected him once, but we won't return upon that. 'I think he must have something important to tell me. Excuse me a minute.' In a little while he returned in haste, and said: 'I find I must say "Good-bye"; there is some business I must attend to on the Flags;' by which name Ainsworth knew the quadrangle of the Exchange was meant. 'I daresay you'll be seeing the governor and all of them soon. Remember me to them. Bye-bye.'

That was the last Ainsworth saw of the triumphant George, and the picture dwelt in his memory.

In an hour he was walking with his friend to the Central Station. As they entered upon the platform, a group of three strange creatures arrested their attention: Daniel Trichinopoly in his white turban and his black alpaca coat—underneath which shone his red cummerbund; a Parsee, fat of feature and of form, topped with his notable brimless Parsee hat; and a grotesque, hideous creature in ordinary English dress, whose face made one think he must have been buried and dug up again when partly decayed, and whom Ainsworth's friend recognised as a Greek or Levantine, well-known as a frequenter of the Flags. They were engaged in serious converse; and Ainsworth wished that George Suffield could see them so; for even the best of men may desire to show himself justified in his suspicions, to say, 'Didn't I tell you so?'

'Don't they look a sinister and villainous trio!' exclaimed Ainsworth. 'Did you ever see three men together that looked liker a conspiracy of evil? What are they talking about, I wonder? Something wicked with money in it, I'll be bound!'

His friend suggested that the man in the white turban looked a simple, honest, good-natured creature.

'Look at that hard, glittering eye!' said Ainsworth. 'It's as cruel as a snake's! I should not be surprised to discover he was the greatest scoundrel of the three. I dislike the looks of the others, but I distrust him upon instinct!'

So he entered the train and returned whence he had come in the morning. When he left the train, he did not need to leave the station, for his luggage was already there in waiting for his journey to London. He turned on the platform to survey his fellow-passengers, wondering if the wearer of the white turban was among them. He was— along with the fat Parsee.

'It is odd,' said he to himself as he saw them walk away together, 'that that is the very combination I guessed when I saw the turbaned scoundrel in Suffield's mill.'

CHAPTER XIV

THE FATTED CALF

THE morning after Isabel found her father she woke early with the horror of the opium den upon her, and she began to reflect what was to be done with him. All day, at school, when not engrossed with her teaching, she considered what arrangements she could make for his comfort and reclamation— yes, reclamation; she did not like to think the word in regard to her father, but she did not know any other (nor do I) that would cover the necessities of his case. She pondered one plan after another, but she finally returned to that of which she had first thought: she must bring her father to live with her. She saw that if she did not she could not properly tend and control him. She was not unaware what that decision might entail upon her—what anxiety, what risk, and what loss even ; but yet she returned to it, and that not merely from an impulsive sentiment. She perceived clearly enough that such a habit as her father's, maintained more or less for twenty years and longer, must not only have ' shattered ' his nerves— as Mr. Doughty declared—but also have sapped his will and ruined his self-respect ; and that, therefore, to restore him to himself would be both an onerous and a tedious task, demanding tact, resource, and patience— in a word, demanding Love. She perceived, also, certain side-issues likely to arise from her contemplated action : her father might (probably would) sometimes break away from her control, cause disquiet in their lodging, and bring upon her more expense than she

could well bear; and her uncle—both her
uncles—might become alienated from her, at
least for a time. And why should she take
this burden upon her? Because it was her
duty?—because he was her father? Not
altogether. Isabel was a young lady of the
kind that the forces of education are tending
to make increasingly common: she did not
accept an opinion or perform an action
merely because tradition or convention said
it was right; she sought to prove all things,
and at the same time to hold fast to that
which is good. She had concluded long ere
this that, as loosely and foolishly applied,
‘ Duty means something disagreeable which
other people think you ought to do; ’ and if
she had thought the particular line of conduct that lay before her disagreeable, and if
she were driven to argue about it, she might
have shown sufficiently that it was not her
bounden duty to rescue her father from the

fate to which he had committed himself, since she owed him nothing but her being. But she had not troubled to argue so—indeed, like a true woman, she had attained her conclusion not at all by course of argument—she merely did not herself think of the word 'Duty' in connection with her father, and would have resented its use by another. The fact that her father was her father inclined her to him, and the discovery that he had something about him which pleased and charmed her made her inclination into positive attraction. In spite of his appearance, in spite of all, she liked him, and she thought well of him; but it is probable she would not have turned her energies with such generosity and alacrity to his resuscitation and rehabilitation, had she not believed him to be a man of talent and attainment.

When school was over she hurried away to her lodging to begin the fulfilment of her purpose. She inquired of her landlady if there was an unoccupied bedroom in the house. Yes; there was a bedroom—'the second-floor back'—recently vacated by a young gentleman that kept late hours.

'Almost as late hours as yourself, miss,' said the landlady pointedly.

'It would probably suit me,' said Isabel, ignoring her allusion. She added on an impulse of mischief: 'It is for a gentleman I should want it, Mrs. Wiffin.'

'Lawk-a-daisy me, miss!' exclaimed Mrs. Wiffin, subsiding into a chair, with her hands limp in her lap. 'The flurries and the worrits you put me into!—you do, indeed! A gentleman! P'raps you're thinking of getting married. But the ways of gentlefolk must be changed. When I was a girl you'd ha' no more thought of having your intended to live in the same house with you than—— There! Well! You're a good, clever, innocent young lady, I believe ; but take my word for it, men are all bad when they get the chance ! And you're a handsome, fine figure of a girl, my dear, and no mother to tell you things !—as I often think to myself when I'm waiting up for you at night.'

'You are a dear, good soul, Mrs. Wiffin,' laughed Isabel, sitting down and taking her landlady's hand, ' and I shall try not to flurry and worry you any more.'

'There's a dear!' said Mrs. Wiffin, patting her hand. 'You see I'm so perceptible to things that touch my feelings.'

Then Isabel revealed to Mrs. Wiffin, as a secret that must be kept from everyone, that it was for her father she desired the extra room : he was in poor health and must be kept quiet, and therefore she wished to take charge of him ; at all which Mrs. Wiffin expressed her surprise and admiration.

She had just sat down to have—as women

foolishly will—a make-shift meal, when there was a loud rat-tat-tat at the street door, and her uncle—Uncle Harry—was shown into her little sitting-room.

'Ah, there you are,' said Uncle Harry. 'I'm restless. I've had a walk across the park, and I thought I'd just have a cup of tea and a chat with you, my dear.'

'It is good of you, uncle, to drop in like this,' said Isabel.

'In this soft London air,' said Uncle Harry, stirring the cup of tea which his niece handed him, 'I am beginning to find I have a liver. I never knew before I had one; but, I suppose, that rascal Daniel's curries—of which I have eaten too many— have developed it.'

'And how,' laughed Isabel, 'do you propose to get rid of your liver, uncle?'

'"By strict regimen," the doctor says, "and by exercise;" by eating and drinking,

that is to say, what I don't like, and by walking more than is comfortable or even possible
in London streets and back-gardens.'

'Don't you think, uncle,' said Isabel with
a smile, ' a homœopathic treatment would
be better ? Eat and drink what you like—
curry or whatever it may be—but in small
doses.'

'Gad!' said he, ' that's a good suggestion—
homœopathic!' And he smiled most agree-
ably, his eyes being involved in good-natured
wrinkles. 'You're a very clever girl, you
know.'

Since he had sat down, it was inevitable
that she should have his brother—her father
—in her thought. ·And still as she looked at
him, and observed the varying expression of
his face, she noted how like he was to his
brother, and yet how unlike : they were, she
said to herself, as a complete personality cleft
in two—Uncle Harry being as the male half,

hard and alert; and her father being as the female, soft, sensuous, and plastic.

' Uncle Harry,' said she, ' have you ever known any one who had for years been addicted to a subtle and insidious kind of poison ? '

' Drink, do you mean ? ' asked Uncle Harry, frowning.

' Something like that,' said she.

' I've known tens—hundreds,' said he.

' What would you do with a person of that sort ? '

' I'd let him drink himself dead,' said Uncle Harry ; ' it's all you can do.'

' Nonsense, uncle,' said Isabel. ' There's surely no habit but can be changed so long as you have a body and a mind. Suppose you wanted to cure a person of that kind, how would you treat the person ? '

' Cut off the liquor at once,' said Uncle Harry.

'Don't you think,' said Isabel, 'that the homœopathic way would be better? Your way seems to me so sudden and dangerous. The person who gets into the habit of drinking to excess, for instance, drinks because of his craving for a stimulant; if you wish to cure him, should not your procedure be first to vary the stimulant?'

'My experience has been,' said Uncle Harry, 'that a man takes drink because he likes it.'

'Likes the effect,' said Isabel, 'which is stimulative, less or more.' Then, continuing her exposition of her view, she went on: 'First vary the stimulant. For instance, in place of dreadful, strong spirits, give him light wine, and good, stimulating food. A person that is given to drinking to excess seldom eats much—does he?'

'Very seldom; never, I may say. As I

heard a soldier once put it, " He eats his beer." '

' Very well ; get your person to eat well ; that will be a new form of stimulation for him. Then gradually divert his attention from these gross and unwholesome forms of stimulation to others of a refined and whole-some nature : to music—if your person is that way inclined—and so on.'

Perceiving the pertinacity with which his niece followed out this exposition, Uncle Harry observed her closely—not exactly with won-der, but with the question in his mind, ' Yes, of course ; but why such steadfast earnestness in this ? '

Isabel, seeing his intent look, and suspect-ing what might be in his thought, dropped her inquiry, saying, ' After all, speculation of that kind is foolish—is it not ? '

' Speculation,' said he sententiously, ' is neither wise nor foolish in itself, but only in regard to the actions it may lead to.'

Having thus closed that discussion, he said, in a manner meant to be very cordial, that he had come on purpose to have a chat about something else; and Isabel, in a tone likewise meant to be very cordial and affectionate, begged to know what it was, while she feared, with a glance at the clock, that she would be much later than she had intended to be in setting out to her father. He was very comfortable, he said, with George and Joanna; he had pitched his tent in their back garden; but he had come to think he would like a 'pitch' of his own; he did not like his · daily view of other people's back windows, and he did not like to order about other people's servants. Isabel thought —with her eye on the clock—that it would be very lonely for him to live by himself. Naturally, he said with a laugh; but he feared he bored his niece; he would come to the point: he had his eye on a companion— oh dear, no! he did not mean marriage— nothing so foolish as that—but yet he meant a lady. And still Isabel furtively eyed the clock.

'It's you I mean,' he said suddenly. 'Would it trouble you—do you think?—to join hands with me?—to live with me? I'm sometimes crotchety, cranky, and crusty, I believe; but you're a sensible girl, and you could manage me, I've no doubt. I think we should suit each other. What do you say, my girl?'

'You are very kind, uncle,' said she quietly, very much astonished and per- plexed, and becoming pale under her uncle's shrewd, expectant gaze; she now perceived her difficult position. 'The kindness of your proposal is overwhelming. But I—I think I had better remain as I am.'

' Oh,' said he, with an involuntary snap like the closing of a box. He frowned a little in evident vexation. 'You like your independence, I suppose, and your freedom?'

' It's not that, uncle. No, no; it's not that. I am, believe me, not so enamoured of my independence and freedom. Sometimes they are a trouble and a burden, for, you see, I am a woman—to my great regret.'

' Oh, what is it, then?' asked he, softening his heart again and leaning with a smile over the table. 'Come now; speak to me as you would to a father. Tell me frankly.'

' Frankly, then, uncle,' said Isabel, ' a week ago I would have accepted your proposal gladly, gratefully.'

' A week ago!' said he, leaning back again. 'I see, I see. You think I was unjust to you at first, and now you won't accept any of my kindness. Don't you think that is rather—well, *mean*?—though it is not a word I should have thought of applying to you.'

'Oh, uncle, pray do not think that!" she cried. 'It would indeed be mean if that were my reason! Don't I know how very kind your offer is?—don't I see that you are thinking more of me than of yourself in making it? And I confess that three days ago even I would have welcomed your generosity; it *is* generous and good of you, and it pains me very much to say I can't accept it now. That may seem to you strange; but something has happened within the last day or two, and I have undertaken a responsibility which I cannot lay aside, and which demands that I should live as I am.'

Her uncle wrinkled and puckered his brows in disappointment and suspicion, and drummed on the table. 'I suppose,' said he, 'you would say it is no business of mine to ask the nature of the responsibility?'

'No, no, uncle; I would not say anything of the kind—indeed, I would not! I cannot really tell you, but not because I think it impertinent in you to ask. I may tell you some day—by-and-by—but I cannot tell you now. Pray believe me, uncle.'

'I do believe you, my dear,' said he, patting the hand she extended to him. 'And I believe you are too sensible and clever not to have a sufficient reason for what you are doing, and for keeping it to yourself. Do not trouble yourself. Be good. But I suppose this responsibility won't remain on you for ever? When it's gone, will you promise me to consider my offer?'

'I cannot say how long the responsibility may remain; but it may modify itself; in any case, I promise.'

Then Uncle Harry rose to go. 'I daresay,' said he, 'you feel scarcely equal to a walk this afternoon. You look a little upset, and had better rest, perhaps. If,' he continued, holding her hand and looking at her kindly, 'you should want to confide in me by-and-by about any difficulty, you will not find me backward to help you.'

'You are very good, uncle,' said she; 'and I may come to you for advice by-and-by.'

When he was gone, she turned her thought again to her father with a new cheerfulness and prospect. If she could contrive to reconcile the brothers, might not they yet live, all three, in happy concord? But she could not yet attempt to bring them together; she must first know her father better and effect considerable improvement in his health and conduct. At present she must act, and neither speculate nor dream. She arrayed herself with care—for she felt it would be an advantage with her father to please his eye—and then went out to take the train to King's Cross. When she left that station she made several purchases, and then entered the 'bus for New North Road. Arrived there, she looked about for a fishmonger's ; and having given an order she went on to her father.

When she was over against Mrs. Ackland Snow's she was met by Mr. Doughty, newly shaved and brushed. He made her an elegant bow, and walked on by her side, halting a little on his stick. His conversation was impressive, solemn, and somewhat lugubrious. The chief had spent a bad, restless night, and so had he. Had her father, Isabel asked, eaten well? He had eaten the usual ' meal of resistance ' about two o'clock—an overdone chop, and little else. But what Mr. Doughty chiefly wished to utter at the moment was his unbounded gratitude for what Miss Raynor, he was morally certain, intended to do for her father. He loved and revered the chief—he had been with him for more than twenty years in all variations of temperature and weather—and all he asked for himself was that he might not be completely cut off from the society of the chief, that he might be allowed occasionally to see and speak with him.   And yet another boon he asked.

'I have had a scene with the chief,' said he.   'He wished to know how you found him out, and he asked me full in the face if I had written to you.   With his eyes on me I could not prevaricate, as, I confess, I had intended to do; it is an astonishing thing that you *cannot* prevaricate to those eyes of his.   I admitted I had written to you.   Do not, I beg of you, let him learn that I have written oftener than once; for he would never forgive me if he knew.'

As Isabel entered the little parlour, she saw her father sitting where she had left him the night before, wrapped in an old overcoat, and reading a book.   When he rose to greet her, she perceived that he looked gray and pinched with fatigue; and she noted, moreover, that her appearance had called forth in him a dim gush of tender emotion, which passed upon his countenance like a breath upon a mirror. He appeared shyer with her than he had been the night before, and she felt—as only a woman can subtly feel—that he regarded her presentment with distinct approval.

'I knew you would come,' said he, taking both her hands in his, 'but I did not expect to see you so early. Will you excuse me for a minute?'

He retired into an inner room, and Isabel laid aside her hat and jacket, turned to Mr. Doughty in haste, and begged his assistance in setting forth the table. Mr. Doughty was appalled; for there was, as he said, 'a precarious and perplexing litter' on the table of books and papers. The table was at length cleared, however; and with the aid of a girl tempted up from the basement, who smiled on Isabel in surprise and admiration, the cloth was duly laid. Mr. Doughty's spirits gradually rose, till when Isabel had set out a fowl all ready cooked, bread and butter, and a lettuce and herbs for a salad, and had exhibited a bottle of Burgundy and asked him to draw the cork, he exclaimed: 'Really, Miss Raynor, you appear to me to have made provision for a feast of Apicius!'

There were no wine-glasses to be found; but Isabel thought tumblers would do, and Mr. Doughty readily agreed with her; and delicately and lovingly, with just the proper twist, like a father drawing his child's tooth, he drew the cork of the Burgundy.

'Please, 'm,' said the little maid-servant, bursting in, all aglow with excitement, 'here's the winkles!'

'The winkles?' exclaimed Isabel.

'Yass, 'm. The boy's jes' bring 'em from

the fish-shop!—on a tray!—such a lot! They
do look nice !'

'Oh, the oysters,' said Isabel, and went
with a dish to receive them.

'Oysters !' exclaimed Mr. Doughty as she
went out. 'Let me see; how long is it since
the chief and I have tasted an oyster ?'

At that instant the chief himself re-entered,
clean and clothed, and stood in surprise. He
did not speak, but his bright eye—bright and
open as a child's—quickly compassed the
meaning of the display. When his daughter
reappeared, bringing in the oysters, tears
sprang to his eyes. 'You should not have
done this,' he said. 'It is very good of you,
but we ate abundantly a few hours ago ; did
we not, Alexander ?'

'We did,' answered Mr. Doughty—' sump-
tuously ;' but he added the saving phrase,
' for us.'

' Abundance is relative, father—is it not?'

said Isabel with a bright smile. 'But we can talk of that by-and-by. Discussion may, but oysters must not, be kept waiting. Let us sit down and eat, father. Mr. Doughty, will you look after the wine? You understand it.'

She shrewdly guessed her father liked the turn of her phrases, and she had assurance of that when, surveying her deliberately with pride and pleasure, he said, 'I believe you are a very clever girl, my dear. And I have a conviction that a new epoch in my life has begun.' He pressed her hand, and a tear again moistened his eye.

'Now let us eat,' said she.—'No vinegar for me, thank you,' she remarked presently to Mr. Doughty. 'I prefer their native flavour.'

'"Native flavour,"' said her father, 'is a good phrase—doubly good.'

'It is certainly "doubly good,"' crackled Mr. Doughty; 'for it includes——'

'Oh, pray, Alexander,' exclaimed Mr. Raynor, ' do not explain why !—My excellent friend Alexander, my dear,' said he to his daughter, 'has a poor opinion of the human understanding ; he always spreads his meaning out in plain, large type.—Really, my dear,' he went on, ' these oysters are extremely good. They help to demonstrate that " Appetite doth grow by what it feeds on." '

' Which is more than can be said—is it not ?—for your usual diet, father,' said she. ' Your diet is commonly too abstemious, I believe.'

' No, my dear,' said he; ' I think not. No ; we have pretty fairly divided our tastes between the flesh-pots of Egypt and the onions, the leeks, and the garlic—have we not, Alexander ? '

' I would exclude the leeks and the garlic,

sir,' said Alexander; 'they did not, I believe, come in our way.'

'You are literal, Alexander,' said Mr. Raynor.

'I hope,' said his daughter, 'they were at least well-cooked.'

'No, Miss Raynor,' said Mr. Doughty with feeling, 'they were very ill-cooked indeed, I assure you.'

'That's a pity,' said she; 'for good food well-cooked is the source of most of the virtues of men.'

'My dear,' said her father, considering her again with a smile of delight, 'you are a very clever girl, but you appear to have taken up with a very materialistic philosophy.'

Thus their talk went on in an apparently aimless fashion, though Isabel, for her part, had a distinct end in view. She had quickly perceived that talk—bright, easy talk—was more to her father than meat and drink, and she had resolved to indulge his taste to the best of her ability, even as she had already determined—will he, nill he—to feed him with nourishing food—all that she might have complete influence with him and gradually build him up again into the stature of a man. Her father well said that she was a clever girl.

So they talked, and Isabel all the while kept a watchful eye on her father's plate and glass. When they were nearly empty she did not ask him if he would take more, but she quietly replenished them, so that he was not aware what she was about. It was only when his plate was quite cleared and his glass empty—when the salad was all eaten, and the wine all drunk, and when there remained nothing of the fowl but a dismembered skeleton —it was only then that he came to himself.

'The food you have provided, my dear,' said he, ' has a magical effect. I do not seem to have taken much meat and drink, but yet I feel like him who " on honey-dew hath fed, And drunk the milk of Paradise."—But now let us talk of our plans.'

CHAPTER XV

PLANS AND PROSPECTS

Mr. Raynor left the table and sat in his old easy-chair. 'Let us see,' he said resolutely. 'Of course, my dear, you cannot come and stay here. I think this household is not conceived on such a scale as would admit of it; and the cooking is not good; certainly,' he added with a reflective eye on the table, 'it is not good; and the beds are not soft enough for a lady to lie on.'

'I like a hard bed, father,' said Isabel, humouring his bent.

'You would not like our hard beds here. They are not merely hard—they are rocky. Why, mine often feels to me like a pavement of cobble-stones.   I lie down a man, and rise up a bruise.   No, this house won't do.— Alexander, we must find other and better rooms.   We shall require three bedrooms and a sitting-room, or even a couple of sitting-rooms—a larger and a smaller.   I think it might be a good idea to inquire the rent of a flat, Alexander.   What do you think?'

'I will inquire, sir,' said Alexander, 'if you desire me to.'

'Now, what rent do you think we can afford, Alexander?   Give me a sheet of paper and a pencil—will you.'

Alexander found these articles, and handed them solemnly to him while he continued talking.   He reckoned that he and Alexander could earn five hundred pounds a year; Alexander suggested it would be better to say four, but his chief did not agree with him; for, when you are once about it, five is as easy to get as four.   So he seriously set

himself to calculate on this imaginary basis
of income what amount might be disbursed
for rent, what for food for three people—and
a domestic—and what for clothes and pocket-
money.   And Isabel sat and listened ; she
understood her father better than before, and
she now perceived how little able he must
ever have been to take care of himself and
to battle with the world.   'And yet,' she said
to herself, 'how sensible he is in his imagin-
ings !—and how well he means, the dear
father !—and how generous he would be if
he could !'   It was, of course, perfectly plain
that he intended now to assume the responsibility of his daughter and all her needs—he
even presently hinted that it would be well
so to regulate expenditure that something
considerable might be put by every year to
make a marriage portion for her—and Isabel
had not the heart to show that she doubted
very much whether any income—to speak of

—would be earned by him. She let him think—she believed it would be good for him to think—that he was now about to keep his daughter, and that she was dutifully going to accept his protection.

'You do not ask me, father,' she said, 'if I have any views on this matter.'

'Yes, sir,' said Mr. Doughty readily. 'You had better listen to what Miss Raynor may have to say. She is quite as wise in these matters—perhaps wiser—than we are.'

'Certainly, my dear, certainly,' said he. 'Forgive me;' and he prepared to give instant heed to what she might say.

'I would like to point out, father,' said Isabel, 'that before we can occupy a flat we must have a tolerable amount of furniture, which will cost a good deal of money at once.'

'True, my dear,' said her father humbly;

'I had not thought of that. I perceive my lapse of actuality.'

'Therefore,' continued Isabel with inexorable logic, 'we cannot think of occupying a flat for some time. If we try to find nice furnished rooms—that, too, would take some time.'

'Would it, Alexander?' asked her father.

'Some time, certainly,' answered Alexander.

'Now, I have a plan which will work till something better is got ready,' pursued Isabel. 'I cannot come to you here, father, but you can come to me. I have lodgings in a very nice house, and I can arrange for rooms for you and Mr. Doughty. That would entail no delay; for you can come at once.'

'At once!' exclaimed her father, turning pale at the thought of having to take immediate action. '"At once," my dear, is very sudden!'

'To-morrow, then,' said Isabel; and, though exciting, that suggestion did not seem so disquieting as the other; he was prepared to discuss it. 'Let us talk about it, my dear,' said he. He doubted whether the landlady would like it; and he doubted 'the equity and prudence' of so sudden a move; and so on.

Isabel was good-naturedly ready to discuss it as much and as frequently as he liked; but she had made up her mind that her father should come to her on the morrow—she would arrange with Mr. Doughty to bring him—for she clearly perceived that he, if left to himself, would discuss the matter subtly and casuistically over and over again—and never stir.

When Isabel left her father it was about nine o'clock. She rode from the New North Road to King's Cross outside the omnibus; for the night was warm and fine, being well into June, and the interior of the 'bus would, she knew, be unbearable. She was in high spirits when she set out, with the prospect of success in her mission to her father, and her elevated ride raised them still higher. The air was bland and cool, and the view which spread before her as she descended Pentonville Hill, with the gorgeous, transfused, smoky effect of a London sunset behind the distant pinnacled mass of St. Pancras Station, some-how encouraged hope. The world appeared to her very beautiful; even the world of sordid houses and swarming men and women and children around her was glorified by the mysteries of Life and Love. Her thoughts, of course, mainly dwelt on her father, but, by a subtle and—at first sight—not very apparent connection, they also embraced Alan Ainsworth. She had been led to think of him a good deal during the last day or two, mainly by the coincidence that he, too, was a journalist, as her father was, or had been. Her knowledge of Alan Ainsworth, also, suggested to her the kind of alert, sensitive being her father must have been in the Spring of his days, and bound the two together in a common interest in her mind. If the two only knew each other, what a pleasant association it would be! She imagined them sitting over against her, and discussing all things of interest on earth and in heaven—Literature and Art, 'Faith and Free-will, Foreknowledge absolute.' And the best was that she did not put away this picture as impossible of realisation, because she knew that Ainsworth was coming to London, and that sooner or later she must meet him.

Science has had much to say lately concerning the circumambient ether—that it is the subtle medium for the transmission of light and heat, that it is, probably, the element of electricity, and so forth. If the wonderful ether be all that, if it vibrate with light and heat, why should it not vibrate with love, which is of the essence of heat and light combined ? Why should it not subtly vibrate and communicate between one heart and another ? It is certain that at the same moment when Isabel Raynor was thinking of Alan Ainsworth, Alan Ainsworth was thinking of her—though it must be admitted he had more sedulously thought of her during the last day or two than she had thought of him. He was in London, and had got to work. He had been very much occupied, but yet he had found time to hang about the College for Ladies and the neighbourhood where he knew she lodged, on the chance of encountering her. He longed with all his impulsive soul to see her and to talk with her, though he did not know he had anything particular to say. He had written to Suffield as soon as he had arrived in town ; but he had not yet heard from him ; and he waited and longed. On this very evening he had walked out of his lodgings to eat his evening meal at a café at King's Cross. He had eaten his food to the accompaniment of chiming thoughts of work and of Isabel ; and he had walked out with such thoughts still chiming in his mind, when he chanced to look up and see Isabel descending upon him, as it were from above ! Isabel, we know, held a return ticket from King's Cross to Baker Street, and she stood for an instant on the pavement in hesitation whether to descend into the sulphurous atmosphere of the Underground or to sacrifice her ticket and walk the remainder of the way. She stood thus when she became aware of a tall man regarding her from a step or two off. As soon as her eye lighted on him, the tall man smiled and approached with his hand out. It was Alan Ainsworth.

'So we have met again,' said he. 'I am

very glad. I have been hoping to meet you; but London is such a great place everybody that lives in it seems to revolve in a wider orbit than usual, so that it may take years to cross a friend's course. We will get jostled about if we stand here. Which way are you going, Miss Raynor?'

'I am on my way home to my lodgings,' said she; 'and I was just considering, when I saw you, if I should go by train or walk.'

'Oh, walk—please walk,' said he; 'that is, if it is not too far, and if I may accompany you.'

'It is not so very far,' she answered quietly, though she perceived his eagerness and delight, and though these feelings in him gave a nameless delight to herself. 'My rooms are near Baker Street. But I would not like to take you out of your way; and you may be busy.'

'My way lies westward too; and I am not

busy—and even if I were, that would not matter. I have been wishing to meet you, and I've met you.'

'But,' said she with a smile, 'you have not been long in London, have you?'

'Two days,' he answered—'two whole days. I came up sooner than I had intended. A good post was offered to me, if I could enter upon its occupation at once. My late chief let me off; he has been very good to me. I have discovered since I came up that it was he that got me this offer. He has so overwhelmed me with kindness, that I have been wondering whether I have behaved quite well to him.'

'What?' said Isabel. 'You think he has deliberately set himself to heap coals of fire on your head?' And she looked at him mischievously.

'Oh no,' said he, suffused with her look. 'I don't mean that. But I fear I am very

egotistical—I have not asked you about yourself and your fortunes.'

' Oh,' said she with a laugh, ' my fortunes
are not like yours : they are without excitement. My life swings quietly—for the most
part '—with a reservation in her mind concerning the past day or two—' between my
lodgings and school, school and my lodgings.
I suppose, then, you are now established as a
London journalist. I hope you have done
well for yourself in leaving Lancashire.'

' I am assistant-editor and leader-writer on
the " Evening Banner," and my late chief has
even recommended me for the theatres on
the " Nonesuch," which is, as you know, a
slogging weekly.'

' He seems, indeed, to be taking a kindly
vengeance on you. What else has he done ? '
she asked with a smile. ' Has he not begged
you to be so good as to take his own
place ? '

'No,' said he. 'I will talk no more about myself. I have given myself away to you '— and he laughed, partly because of the ambiguity of his sentence—'but I did not guess you were an ironical person.'

'Did you not?' said she. 'Is it wicked to be ironical?'

'No, no,' said he; 'but if you absolutely decline to speak of yourself, lest I should be ironical, tell me about your uncles. Mr. Suffield has not delighted them yet, I see, with his voice in Parliament; but Mr. Raynor has lectured at the Royal Geographical. You went to the lecture, of course?'

Thus they talked as they walked along the Euston Road. Arrived at the corner of Euston Square by the St. Pancras Church with its absurd caryatides, he stopped a moment and pointed down Woburn Place. '*My* lodgings,' said he, 'are down there. They are handy for the office and for the Reading

Room of the British Museum. Do you ever go to the Reading Room?'

'No,' she answered, again with a spice of mischief; for a woman is never so irrestrainably mischievous as when she is pleased with her companion. 'Why should I go? I am not a literary person at all.'

'You might be if you liked,' said he; 'but I am glad you are not.'

'Why?' she asked. 'Does your assistant-editorial highness not approve of female writers? Would you like to keep writing a close guild for men?'

'Oh no,' he answered to the accompaniment of a fine frank blush; being but a mere blundering male creature, he wondered at the sharpness of her speech while he liked it. 'I have no opinion on the question in general; I have only a feeling as to particular instances. I have met a few women that write, and I had rather not meet them again—that's all.'

Then there began to flow in the mind of each a current of speculation and desire beneath the matters to which they were apparently giving their attention and of which they were talking. 'Here,' thought Ainsworth, ' is the pleasantest, sweetest, most delightful comrade a man could have—pleasanter, sweeter far than any male comrade ; and yet, I suppose I must be cut off from her society except on certain precise and formal occasions, when I may meet her in a company! I cannot ask her to drop in and see me ; and she cannot—even if she wishes it— ask me to drop in and see her. Mrs. Grundy and propriety forbid it, because she is a lone woman and I am a lone man !' At the same time Isabel was thinking that she had not known Ainsworth quite so frankly and buoyantly boyish before. Was it the sense of being in a wilderness of men and women who did not care one jot for his existence that gave him that touch of naïve, irresponsible youthfulness? However it was, she liked his buoyancy and his boyishness, and she said to herself: ' How he would delight in my father! —and how my father would delight in him! How much good they might do each other! How stimulating each might be to the other! And yet I cannot bring them together! Can I? Can I not? Why not? Why not, indeed? Am I ashamed of my father? Do I propose to keep him always hidden? And if I do not, why should I not show him at once, at least to Mr. Ainsworth, who, I am sure, will neither misunderstand him nor me?' It is a very subtle and seductive experience that —the sure and certain feeling—which is more frequently based on intuition and understanding than on reason and knowledge—that there is one person who will never misunderstand or mistake you whatever you may say or do; it is very closely akin to a fuller experience which Isabel had as yet no notion she was beginning to undergo.

Isabel, as we have seen, was a young lady who, when she had decided that a course was right, did not review and re-review her decision, and thus postpone action till the ebb of feeling.

' Mr. Ainsworth,' said she, 'have you ever heard me speak of my father ? '

' Your father ? ' exclaimed Ainsworth. 'I did not know you had a father ! I mean, of course, that I had always supposed he was dead.'

' He has been virtually dead for many years—dead to me and to my aunt and uncles since I was a baby. Some other time I will tell you all about it. " He was dead, but is alive again," ' she said, quoting but half-consciously the sacred words; ' " he was lost and is found." Yesterday I found him; I am just come from him now ; and I am going to bring him to live with me—without, for the present, telling my uncles or my aunt anything about it.'

'It is very noble, and beautiful, and filial of you!' said Ainsworth.

'No, no,' said she; 'it is not. Don't use such absurd adjectives. I am merely doing it because I like to do it.'

'But,' said he, 'though it is not for me to question what you propose to do, may I suggest that you may not have considered all the trouble and—and distress that it may entail?'

'I have considered all that,' said she. 'I know what you are thinking of. But he is not a bad man, or a gross man. He is a clever, gentle creature—my poor father!—simple, weak, and docile as can be. You remember Coleridge and his besetting weakness? Well, my father is something like Coleridge. The habit that has ruined him is the same, and his cleverness is of the same kind too. He is coming to me to-morrow, and I want to ask you to do me a favour: come and see him sometimes, and talk to him. He is very interesting, I think; he used to be an editor, and he writes still a little, and he and you may find each other good company; at any rate, I am sure it will cheer and encourage him to find a young man interested in him.'

'My dear Miss Ràynor,' said Ainsworth—and in his impulsive fervour he had to put a restraint on himself not to seize and press Isabel's hand; he grasped and pressed his own instead—'whatever I can do, I will do; but do not use the word "favour" in connection with it. It will be a precious privilege to please you, and to do anything for your father.'

'Thank you,' said she simply; his fervour made her somewhat shy. 'I am hoping,' she continued, ' to cure him gradually of his habit.'

' You will,' exclaimed Ainsworth in the fullest belief—' you will!'

' And, of course,' said she, ' you understand that all this is for the present a secret.'

' I understand,' said he. ' And—and I appreciate your having taken me into your confidence.'

' This,' said she, stopping at a little gate—the number of which Ainsworth eagerly noted—' is where I lodge. Good-bye.'

She gave him her hand and smiled frankly on him, so that he was penetrated through and through with delight. He looked back after he had turned away, and at the same instant she glanced over her shoulder. She smiled and nodded to him, and he raised his hat and went on, ravished with her charm. Never, he thought, had there been so spirited a poise of head and neck as that she showed when she turned; never, certainly, had he seen so divine and enthralling a smile—a smile that had been all for him!—and never, surely, had there been in all the world a kinder, sweeter, more fascinating, or more beautiful woman than she! The red gold of sunset was glowing behind him as he walked away, and he murmured to himself:

> Rosy is the West, rosy is the South;
> Roses are her cheeks, and a rose her mouth!'

END OF THE FIRST VOLUME

www.ingramcontent.com/pod-product-compliance
Lightning Source LLC
Chambersburg PA
CBHW020930120726
47905CB00008B/2462